A TOOL
FOR UNDERSTANDING
HUMAN DIFFERENCES

A TOOL
FOR
UNDERSTANDING
HUMAN
DIFFERENCES

How To Discover and Develop Your Type According to Dr. C.G. Jung and Dr. William Sheldon

Tyra Arraj and Jim Arraj

Tools for Inner Growth
Box 520
Chiloquin, Oregon 97624

Library of Congress Cataloging in Publication Data

Arraj, Tyra.
   A tool for understanding human differences.

   Bibliography: p.
   Includes index.
   1. Typology (Psychology) 2. Difference (Psychology) 3.Jung, C. G. (Carl Gustav), 1875-1961.
4. Sheldon, William Herbert, 1899-1977. I. Arraj, Jim.
II. Title. BF698.A742 1984   155.2'64   84-91430
ISBN 0-914073-00-1

PRINTED IN THE UNITED STATES OF AMERICA

For Our Parents and Doris

Acknowledgements

We would like to thank all the people who made this book possible: Elizabeth and John, and all our friends who put up with it.

All those who provided information: Billy Arraj, K.W. Bash, Roland Elderkin, C. Jess Groesbeck, J. Robert Hanson, Emil Hartl, Edward Humphreys, Franz Jung, L.H. Knowles, and Miriam Curtis and The William Sheldon Trust, Robert Lenski, Mary McCaulley, Mary McDermott, C.A. Meier, Edward Monnelly, P. O'B. Montgomery, Gene Olson, Humphrey Osmond, George Schemel, Horace Stewart, Ashton Tenney and George Winokur.

Special thanks to: C. Wesley and Helen S. Dupertuis for generously spending time and energy with us, and Betty Emmert and Marguerite Webb who went out of their way to help us obtain much of the research material.

Contents

TABLES

FIGURES

Introduction

A TYPE TOOL

We live in a world of all different kinds of people; they are short and tall, strong and weak, fat and thin, friendly and reserved, enthusiastic and calm, fast and slow, and a thousand other qualities. Somehow we have to get along with them all, and to do this we need a way to understand what makes them different. Imagine if someone invented a tool that could help us sort out these diversities so we could deal with people better. We would certainly want to get our hands on it.

Such a tool actually exists. William Sheldon discovered a way to understand body types, and how they give rise to various temperaments. C. G. Jung pointed out the inner elements of the psyche that combine to form distinct kinds of psychological types. We have put these two typologies together to form one tool, a type tool.

Part I helps you discover your own type.
Part II helps you develop your own type.
Part III is more technical and is written for people who have a professional interest in the field of human differences, as well as for the general reader.

The vital ingredient that is missing in this book is your own personal experience. Types are meant to be used and not simply understood, just as a piano is meant to be played and not simply stand in the living room. Pick up the type tool. Do the self-discovery quizzes. Practice with it and get used to the feel of it, and use it to deepen your insight into yourself and the people around you.

Part I
Discover Your Own Type

Chapter 1

William Sheldon's
Body and Temperment Types

What is a type?

There is something in the very idea of typing people that makes us feel uneasy, even though it doesn't bother us to talk about types of roses or pine trees or human blood. The idea of human types threatens us from two directions. First, we are afraid that it will pigeon-hole us and deny our uniqueness, and replace it with a superficial label. Secondly, we feel it is somehow undemocratic, and fear it could lead to prejudice and repression.

Typology is the study of human differences. Those of William Sheldon and C. G. Jung are not based on set descriptions that real people must be fit into, but on basic elements which, when combined together, can be used to describe the differences among people. A type is a group of characteristics that stands midway between the universal traits common to us all and those which are uniquely our own. For example, we all have eyes. Yet our own eyes are unlike anyone else's. But between these two poles there are groupings of blue-eyed people, brown-eyed people, etc. Types are a bridge between the universal and the particular.

As we shall see, there are body, temperament, and psychological types. Every typology can be abused in order to deny the universal or the unique in man, but a good typology is a powerful aid to deeper understanding of who we are.

Who was Dr. William Sheldon?

William Sheldon, 1898-1977, was an American doctor and psychologist. He grew up with an intimate knowledge of animal

1

breeding from life on his father's farm. He later taught and did research at a number of U.S. universities and is best known for his series of books on the variety of human differences. Sheldon could be called a human naturalist with a tremendous interest in observing the infinite variety of human bodies and temperaments, and out of these extensive observations he gradually elaborated his typology.

The Basic Components of Physique.

For his study of the human physique, Dr. Sheldon started with 4,000 photographs of college-age men, which showed front, back and side views. By careful examination of these photographs he discovered that there were three fundamental elements which, when combined together, made up all these physiques or somatotypes. With great effort and ingenuity he worked out ways to measure these three components and to express them numerically so that every human body could be described in terms of three numbers, and that two independent observers could arrive at very similar results in determining a person's body type. These basic elements he named endomorphy, mesomorphy and ectomorphy, for they seemed to derive from the three layers of the human embryo, the endoderm, the mesoderm and the ectoderm.

Endomorphy is centered on the abdomen, and the whole digestive system.

Mesomorphy is focused on the muscles and the circulatory system.

Ectomorphy is related to the brain and the nervous system.

We each contain all three elements in our bodily make-up, just as we all have digestive, circulatory and nervous systems. No one is simply an endomorph without having at the same time some mesomorphy and ectomorphy, but we have these components in varying degrees. Sheldon evaluated the degree a component was present on a scale ranging from one to seven, with one as the minimum and seven as the maximum.

The Three Body Type Extremes

The Extreme Endomorph—Roundness

Endomorphy

The easiest way to get an idea of the variety of human physiques is by looking at the three extremes, even though in actual life the various combinations are much more common. According to Sheldon's system a 711 (seven-one-one) was the most extreme endomorph with minimal mesomorphy and ectomorphy. In this physique the body is round and soft, as if all the mass had been concentrated in the abdominal area. In fact, the large intestine of an extreme endormorph can be two or three times the length of that of an ectomorph. Sheldon likened this abdomen to a powerful boiler room with fine powers of assimilation. The arms and legs of the extreme endomorph are short and tapering, and the hands and feet comparatively small, with the upper arms and thighs being hammed and more developed than the lower arms and legs. The body has smooth contours without projecting bones, and a high waist. There is some development of the breast in the male and a fullness of the buttocks. The skin is soft and smooth like that of an apple, and there is a tendency towards premature baldness beginning at the top of the head and spreading in a polished circle. The hair is fine and the whole head is spherical. The head is large and the face broad and relaxed with the features blending into an over-all impression of roundness. The head can be likened to a pumpkin sitting on a barrel, and the abdomen to a sphere with the chest attached to it like an inverted funnel.

Sheldon imagined the body of the endomorph as a balloon whose walls were thinner at the abdomen and thicker further away. When the balloon was inflated it was largest at the abdomen and smallest at the farthest extremities. Santa Claus is our society's image of the extreme endomorph.

The Extreme Mesomorph-Muscles

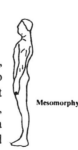

Mesomorphy

In the extremely mesomorphic physique, or 171, thre is a squareness and hardness of the body due to large bones and well-defined muscles. The chest area, which Sheldon likened to an engine room, dominates over the abdominal area and tapers to a relatively narrow, low waist. The bones and

3

muscles of the head are prominent as well, with clearly defined cheek bones and a square, heavy jaw. The face is long and broad and the head tends towards a cubical shape. The muscles on either side of the neck create a pyramid-like effect. Both the lower and upper arms and legs are well-developed and the wrists and fingers are heavy and massive. The skin is thick and tends towards coarseness. It takes and holds a tan well and can develop a leathery appearance with heavy wrinkles. Sheldon compared it to the skin of an orange. The hair is basically heavy-textured, and baldness, when it appears, usually starts at the front of the head. The extreme mesomorph is Mr. Universe or Tarzan.

Sheldon's initial work with body and temperament types was based mostly on males, and it is in the description of the extreme mesomorph that we have the most need to develop a corresponding female mesomorphic description. Women on the whole tend to have less mesopmorphy than men and more endomorphy. Women who are primarily mesomorphs rarely show the same degree of sharp angularity, prominent bone structure and highly relieved muscles found in their male counterparts. Their contours are smoother, yet the chest area clearly dominates over the abdominal area and both upper and lower arms and legs are well-muscled. The skin tends to be finer than in the male mesomorph, but shows some of the same characteristics in terms of tanning and wrinkling.

The Extreme Ectomorph-Linear

The highly ectomorphic physique, or 117, is fragile and delicate with light bones and slight muscles. The limbs are relatively long and the shoulders droop. In contrast to the compactness of the endomorph and mesomorph, the ectomorph is extended in space and linear. The ribs are visible and delicate and the thighs and upper arms weak. The fingers, toes and neck are long. The features of the face are sharp and fragile, and the shape of the face as a whole is triangular with the point of the triangle at the chin. The teeth are often crowded in the lower jaw which is somewhat receding. The skin is dry and is like the outer skin of an onion. It tends to burn and peel easily and not retain a

Ectomorphy

tan. The relatively great bodily area in relation to mass makes the ectomorph suffer from extreme heat or cold. The hair is fine and fast-growing and sometimes difficult to keep in place. Baldness is rare. The extreme ectomorph in our society is the absent-minded professor or Ichabod Crane.

Discovering Your Own Somatotype

There are only a few of us who fit the descriptions of the 3 extreme somatotypes. Most of us are more moderate combinations of the 3 basic elements. Dr. Sheldon has many detailed descriptions of the different somatotypes, but happily for our purposes in making a type tool, we do not need to be so exacting. A more simplified procedure will work for us.

First, what is your strongest component? Is it endomorphy (roundness), or mesomorphy (muscles) or ectomorphy (linear)? Or is it a close tie between 2 or 3 components? Try to mentally weigh each component to see which is heavier or more dominant. Do the self-discovery quiz as an aid in the process of evaluation.

The Body Type Self-Discovery Quiz

Put a check next to the phrase that best describes you. If 2 fit equally well, or even 3, check all that fit. When you are finished, add up the checks and see which element has the most.

	Endomorphy	Mesomorphy	Ectomorphy
My body can best be described as	_round and soft	_square and hard	_long and thin
My shoulders are	_high and smooth	_broad and muscular	_drooping and bony
Someone would call my facial features	_somewhat soft and indistinct	_clear-cut and well-defined	_small and fragile
My neck is	_smooth and round	_fairly long and broad	_long and thin
The shape that best fits my face is	_round	_rectangular	_triangular, with the point at the chin

Continues on p. 6

5

The Body Type Self-Discovery Quiz (Continues)

	Endomorphy	Mesomorphy	Ectomorphy
My lips are	_soft and full	_thick and well-defined	_thin and delicate
My muscles are	_smooth without relief	_rugged and prominent	_slight and underdeveloped
My stomach is	_round and prominent	_compact and muscular	_small and unmuscular
When I compare my upper arm to my lower arm	_the upper is heavier	_both are heavily muscled	_the upper arms are relatively weak and the forearms long
My wrists are best described as	_round	_big and bony	_thin and bony
My hands are	_relatively small	_large and well-muscled	_narrow and long-fingered
My knuckles and joints are	_not distinct	_large and outstanding	_small
My back is	_wide top and bottom	_broad and tapering	_relatively narrow
My buttocks are	_soft and round	_muscular	_thin and un-muscled
My hair is best described as	_fine and manageable	_coarse-textured	_rapid-growing and sometimes unruly
My skin is	_smooth and velvety	_thick	_thin and dry
When I try to get a tan		_it is deep and lasting	_scanty with peeling
My waist is best described as	_high and large	_low and well-muscled	_non-muscular and small

6

Which element is strongest, and what are the 2nd and 3rd choices? For example, a person who is a mesomorphic ectomorph is someone who has a fair degree of muscularity but with a greater degree of ectomorphy. He might be unsatisfied with checking ectomorphy alone because he is attracted to the mesomorphic choice as well. However, he knows that endomorphy is his least developed component, and with some deliberation can decide that ectomorphy is stronger than mesmorphy in his own particular combination of them.

If you experience a great deal of trouble in deciding what component is dominant in your body type it may be due to the fact that two elements are of almost the same strength, or even three elements. For example, the 443 and the 444 are relatively common body types, and in the latter case there are equal degrees of endomorphy, mesomorphy and ectomorphy. In the following diagram the three corners represent the three body type extremes, while the center represents the 444. The area around the center is covered by the other mid-range or balanced body types. Tentatively try to find your own place on the diagram.

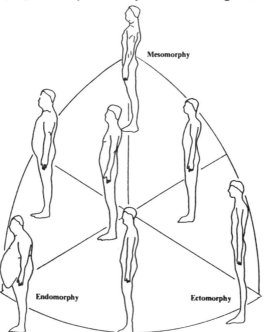

Fig. 1. The Somatotype Chart of Physiques

7

The Basic Components of Temperament

Temperament explores how people eat and sleep, laugh and snore, speak and walk. Temperament is body type in action. Sheldon's procedure in looking for the basic components of temperament was much like the one he used in discovering the body type components. He interviewed in depth several hundred people and tried to find traits which would describe the basic elements of their behavior. He found there were three basic components which he eventually named endotonia, mesotonia and ectotonia.

Endotonia is seen in the love of relaxation, comfort, food and people.

Mesotonia is centered on assertiveness and a love of action.

Ectotonia focuses on privacy, restraint and a highly developed self-awareness.

Sheldon devised a way of numerically rating the strength of each area based on a check-list of 60 characteristics that describe the basic components. The 711 was the extreme endotonic, the 171 the extreme mesotonic and the 117 the extreme ectotonic. He found a strong correspondence between the endomorphic body type and the endotonic temperament, the mesomorphic body type and the mesotonic temperament, and the ectomorphic body type and the ectotonic temperament. Just as in our body type we have all three elements, so, too, with our temperament. A look at the three extremes in temperament will give us some idea of what these components are like.

The Extreme Endotonic-Friendliness

The endotonic shows a splendid ability to eat, digest and socialize. A good deal of his energy is oriented around food, and he enjoys sitting around after a good meal and letting the digestive process proceed without disturbance. Endotonics live far from the upsets and nervous stomachs of the ectotonics. They fall readily to sleep and their sleep is deep and easy; they lie limp and sprawled out and frequently snore.

Endotonics are relaxed and slow-moving. Their breath comes from the abdomen and is deep and regular. Their speech is unhurried and their limbs often limp. They like sitting in a well-upholstered chair and relaxing. All their reactions are slow, and this is a reflection on a temperament level of a basal metabolism, pulse, breathing rate and temperature which are all often slower and lower than average. The circulation in their hands and feet tends to be poor. Sheldon calls these people biologically introverted organisms. It is as if all the energy is focused on the abdominal area, leaving less free to be expressed in the limbs and face, and giving an impression of a lack of intensity.

Sheldon felt that biological introversion gave rise to psychological extraversion. Since the bodies of the endotonics are so focused on the central digestive system, they need and crave social stimulation in order to feel complete on the social level. Groups of people, rather than fatiguing them, stimulate them to the proper level of social interaction. The assimilative powers that on the physical level were oriented to food, now on the social level draw them to people.

The endotonics love to socialize their eating, and the sharing of meals becomes an event of the highest importance. They treat guests well. They love company and feel more complete with other people around. They like people simply because they are people. They have a strong desire to be liked and approved of, and this often leads them to be very conventional in their choices in order not to run the risk of social disapproval. The endotonics are open and even with their emotions which seem to flow out of them without any inhibitions. Whether they are happy or sad, they want the people around them to know about it, and if others express emotion they react directly and convincingly in sympathy. When an endotonic has been drinking he becomes even more jovial and radiates an expansive love of people. Endotonics are family-oriented and love babies and young children and have a highly developed maternal instinct.

In summary, they love assimilation both on the physical and social level. They love to eat and digest, to be part of their family and community, to like and be liked and to rest and relax in these processes of assimilation. They crave food and affection and abhor isolation and disapproval. They express affection and approval readily and need both back in kind.

While it is important to look at the three extremes of physique and the three extremes of temperament because they help us understand the basic components, they can be misleading. There are very few people who embody these extremes without the noticeable influence of the other temperament components. The stories that follow are examples of less extreme types. They are meant to simply be a starting point to encourage you to come up with your own examples.

Harry and Beth: endotonics

Dropping in on Harry and Beth was never any strain. Their house was always busy. There was Harry with a cup of coffee in his hand as a parade of friends, relatives, kids, cats, dogs and no doubt some perfect strangers marched into the kitchen. The strangers didn't maintain that status for more than five minutes. Harry put them at ease with a smooth flow of often hilarious stories while Beth mothered them with an open-hearted friendliness and a piece of pie. They ate, talked, worked, laughed and spent with the same good-natured matter-of-fact attitude. Both Harry and Beth had problems with their weight, their budget and getting their whole bustling busy life organized, and if they occsionally felt down and blue, they would pick up when they had a chance to talk it out.

Sally, an endotonic with mesotonia.

Sally had been big and strong even as a child. In later years she grew heavy, but it was not the heaviness of a large stomach, but a stockiness and massiveness of the whole body. She was an earthy good-natured woman, neither effusive nor sensitive, but steady and warm. She liked to go visiting with a cake under one arm and a bag of doughnuts in the other. She didn't look for thanks in terms of words, but rather a hot cup of coffee to go with the goodies and some time to relax and visit.

Sally's house was a casual clutter of her many possessions. She was open-handed with her money, and loved to buy the latest gadgets and little mechanical wonders, not only for herself but for everyone around her. She didn't get flustered, and this stood her in good stead as a matron of the local jail. She had steady nerves that could confront calamities without flinching, and yet at the same time she had the strength and energy to impose some sort of order on the chaotic situations that she had to confront daily.

At first glance she sometimes appeared brusque and tough, but anyone who had any real contact with her found her warm and easy-going. Her greatest display of feelings were reserved for her own family and relatives, especially in any time of crisis or trouble. With Sally you always knew where you stood.

The Extreme Mesotonic-Action

In endotonia the stomach was the focus of attention, but in

mesotonia it is the muscles. The mesotonic is well-endowed with them, or to put it another way, the mesotonic's muscles seem to have a mind of their own. They are always ready for action, and good posture is natural to them. They get up with plenty of energy and seem tireless. They can work for long periods of time and both need and like to exercise. They like to be out doing things. If they are forced into inactivity they become restless and dejected.

The mesotonic tends to eat his food rapidly and somewhat randomly, often neglecting set meal times. He sleeps the least of the three types and sometimes contents himself with six hours. He is an active sleeper who thrashes about. He shows an insensitivity to pain and a tendency to high blood pressure and large blood vessels.

The mesotonic has no hesitation in approaching people and making known his wants and desires. The tendency to think with his muscles and find exhilaration in their use leads him to enjoy taking chances and risks, even when the actual gain is well-known to be minimal. They can become fond of gambling and fast driving and are generally physically fearless. They can be either difficult and argumentative, or slow to anger, but always with the capacity to act out physically and usually with some sort of history of having done so on special occasions.

This physical drive manifests itself on the psychological level in a sense of competition. The mesotonic wants to win and pushes himself forward. He is unhesitant about the all-out pursuit of the goal he seeks. Associated with this trait is a certain psychological callousness. He tends to walk roughshod over the obstacles in his path and the people who stand in the way of his achieving what he wants. On the positive side this is called being practical and free from sentimentality, but on the negative side it is called ruthlessness or obnoxious aggressiveness.

This outward energetic flow makes mesotonics generally noisy. They bustle about doing things and since their inhibitions are low, the attendant noise does not bother them. Their voices carry and sometimes boom out as if speech were another form of exercise. When alcohol reduces their inhibitions, they become more assertive and aggressive. When trouble strikes they revert to their most fundamental form of behavior and seek action of some sort. Mesotonics tend to glorify that period of youthful activities where physical powers reach their peak, or perhaps more accurately the period of youth that best symbolizes a sense of endless vitality and activity. This glorification of youth goes hand-in-hand with the early maturing of the mesotonic organism, both facially and muscularly. They look older than their chronological age. The extraversion of action that is so strong here goes together with a lack of awareness of what is happening on the subjective level. The quickness with which the mesotonic can make decisions is compensated for by a relative unawareness of the other parts of his personality. He tends to be cut off from his dream life. He likes wide-open spaces and freedom from the restraint of clothes.

As we saw in the case of the mesomorphic physique, Sheldon's portrait of the mesotonic is more male than female. The female mesotonic shows the same extraversion of action, but how this action expresses itself has a different quality. There is not the same overt physical compativeness and competitive aggressiveness. The action is more muted and flows in more socially acceptable channels. The mesotonic woman should be compared not with mesotonic men but with other women, and it is in relationship to other women that she shows the distinctive mesotonic traits in a feminine way.

Bert: a mesotonic with some endotonia

Bert was a long-haul truck driver who had a reputation as a man who got where he set out to go. When the storm warnings went up about snow in the high passes he had a slight grin on his face as he jumped in the cab to see what was really happening up there. No snow had stopped him yet!

Bert figured he had been a bit wild as a young man and gave as good as he got, especially after a few drinks. Now he had settled down, but let some dummy come cutting in front of him and he still saw red. But with a wife and kids a man had to be steadier than when he could just take his pay check and go off to do what he wanted. Bert never really liked to kick back and rest. He would grab a few hours sleep and be off again. It was no good for a man to pamper himself.

Rita: a mesotonic

Rita was a good looking girl with all the curves in the right places, and she knew it. She would spend hours fixing her hair and carefully applying her make-up, and the clothes she wore made her look older than she was. When she came into a room she immediately and almost magically became the center of attention.

She liked the way the older boys would sort of hesitate and stutter a bit when she came right up to them and gave them one of those looks.

Rita was tired of living home. It was so dull when there were so many exciting things you could do if you were out on your own. School was a bore, too, except for the chance to see the gang. Rita got her way most of the time and she felt that was only right. Wasn't she really grown-up for her age?

Sheldon felt that estimating the degree of mesotonia was the most difficult part of evaluating a person's temperament. At times people with well-developed mesotonia can give the surface appearance of exceptional calmness and amiability. This is particularly true of the extreme mesomorphs of above-average height who form a kind of mesomorphic royalty. They expect and get special treatment. Sheldon likened them to big cats who go around with their claws retracted, and only when provoked or in the midst of a crisis does their mesotonia show itself clearly.

The Extreme Ectotonic-Reflection

The outstanding characteristic of the ectotonic is his finely-tuned receptive system. His spread-out body acts like a giant antenna picking up all sorts of inputs. Sheldon calls the ectotonic a biologically extraverted organism, which is compensated for by psychological introversion.

Since the whole organism is sensitive to stimulation, the ectotonic develops a series of characteristic strategies by which he tries to cut down on them. He is like a sonar operator who must constantly be wary of a sudden loud noise breaking in on the delicate sounds he is trying to trace. He likes to cross his legs and curl up as if he is trying to minimize his exposure to the exterior world. He tries to avoid making noise and being subjected to it. He shrinks from crowds and large groups of people and likes small, protected places.

The ectotonic suffers from a quick onset of hunger and a quick satiation of it. He is drawn to a high protein, high calorie diet, with frequent snacking to match his small digestive system. He has a nervous stomach and bowels. He is a quiet sleeper, but a light one, and he is often plagued by insomnia. He tends to sleep on one side with his legs drawn up, and his sleep, though slow in coming, can be hard to shake off. His energy level is low, while his reactions are fast. He suffers from a quasi-chronic fatigue and must protect himself from the temptation to exercise heavily. His blood pressure is usually low and his respiration shallow and rapid with a fast and weak pulse. His temperature is elevated slightly above normal and it rises rapidly at the onset of illness. The ectotonic is resistant to many major diseases, but suffers excessively from insect bites and skin rashes. Unfortunately he can succumb to acute streptococcal infections of the throat which cause swelling and strangulation. His hypersensitivity leads not only to quick physical reactions but to excessively fast social reactions as well. It is difficult for this type to keep pace with slow-moving social chit-chat. He races ahead and trips over his own social feet.

Just as the endotonic loves to eat and the mesotonic loves action, the ectotonic loves privacy. He needs shelter from excessive stimulation and time to sort out the inputs he has received, and connect them up with his own inner subjective experience, which he values highly. Self-awareness is a principle trait of ectotonia. The feelings of the ectotonic are not on display, even though they can be very strong, and so he is sometimes accused of not having any. When they are in a situation of dealing with someone who has authority over them or with someone of the opposite sex whom they are interested in, they often make a poor first impression. They are uncomfortable in coping with social situations where overt expressions of sympathy are called for or where general idle conversation is the norm, for example in parties and dinners where they have no intimate acquaintances.

The ectotonics are hypersensitive to pain because they anticipate it and have a lower pain threshold as well. They do not project their voices like the mesotonics, but focus it to reach only the person they are addressing. They appear younger than their age and often wear an alert, intent expression. They have a late adolescence, consider the latter part of life the best, and are future-oriented. The more extreme ectotonics have a distaste for alcohol and their accentuated consciousness fights alcohol, drugs and anaesthesia and is resistant to hypnosis. They can get in touch readily with their dream life and often nurture a rich fantasy life. When they become troubled they seek privacy and solitude in order to try to work out the difficulty.

Mark: an ectotonic

Mark taught history of religions at the local community college. He had always been a quiet guy and still shied away from faculty parties and student rallies. His social life, such as it was, centered on his home and a small group of friends. He had a general reputation of being intelligent, but too aloof and cold. The people who did get behind the wall of reserve with which he surrounded himself found him an original and creative thinker, and a warm, kind man as well, but basically a very shy and hesitant one when it came to showing his feelings. Mark had married late with real misgivings, for he had always looked at a wife and children as a kind of entrapment that would imprison him in the everyday world.

Discovering Your Own Temperament Type

While there are some people who are close to the temperament type extremes we have described here, most of us are various combinations. Try to figure out what your strongest component of temperament is. Is it endotonia (amiability), mesotonia (action), or ectotonia (reflection)? Or is it a close tie between two or three components? Try to mentally weigh each component to see which has the greatest weight at this level of temperamental behavior. Do the self-discovery quiz as an aid in the process of evaluation.

The Temperament Type Self-Discovery Quiz

Put a check next to the phrase that best describes you. If two fit equally well, or even three, check all that fit. When you are finished, add up the checks and see which element has the most.

	Endotonia	Mesotonia	Ectotonia
My posture and movements are	_relaxed	_assertive	_restrained
If I were to choose what I enjoy most it would be	_physical comfort	_physical adventure	_privacy
When I feel troubled I seek out	_people	_action	_solitude
I look with the most favor on	_childhood and family	_early adulthood	_the later periods of life

15

Continues on p. 16

The Temperament Type Self-Discovery Quiz (Continues)

	Endotonia	Mesotonia	Ectotonia
When I drink alcohol I get	_more relaxed and friendly	_assertive and stick up for my rights	_tired and don't want to continue
People would say that my facial appearance is	_relaxed	_more mature than my age	_younger than my age
My sleep is	_deep	_somewhat active	_easily broken up
The fear that would bother me most would be	_being cut off from other people	_being closed in small spaces	_being exposed to endless noise and company
In the face of pain I		_tend towards indifference	_tend towards hypersensitivity
I am more inclined towards		_letting my voice get loud	_restraining my voice most of of the time
If people were to complain about me they would say I am too	_indiscriminately friendly	_competitive	_inhibited in dealing with other people
The thing I like most is	_eating	_exercise	_time to myself
The trait that would most characterize me is	_a love of affection and approval	_a love of running things	_a high degree of self- awareness and a love of doing things my own way
I enjoy	_having a peaceful time after my meal	_taking chances and risks	_entering a world of my own
When in a group I like most to	_mingle	_take charge	_take off
People would complain I am	_too relaxed	_too assertive	_too anxious
I would most likely be complimented on being	_calm	_energetic	_reflective
I am more inclined to	_allow things to happen	_start things	_observe things
If people were to compliment me they would say I was	_generous	_enterprising	_resourceful

16

Notes on Further Study

The Body Types

The best source of detailed information on body types is to be found in Sheldon's *Varieties of Human Physique* and the *Atlas of Men*. The *Varieties of Human Physique* contains detailed descriptions not only of the three extreme body types or somatotypes, but many others as well. It also describes how Sheldon devised his theory of somatotypes and put it into practice.

The *Atlas of Men*, which contains photographs of over 1,000 different male physiques, is the best tool in gaining an overview of the different somatotypes. In it Sheldon describes one of his earlier methods for estimating the body type, which is based on calculations of height and weight, and the visual inspection of possible physiques to fit these dimensions. There is also an *Atlas of Children* by G. Petersen.

The Temperament Types

The best description of temperaments is to be found in Sheldon's *Varieties of Temperament* which contains six full-length case studies, as well as a more detailed presentation of the material we have used in this chapter.

Quizzes for Body and Temperament Types

A more technical presentation of the kinds of material in the quizzes can be found in the following sources:

Body Type

1. Check list of inspectional criteria (male), p. 37-46 of the *Varieties of Temperament*.

2. P.M. Danby, 1953, "A Study of the Physique of Some Native East Africans," J. Roy. Anth. Inst. 83: 194-214.

Temperament Type

1. The scale for temperament, p. 26, in the *Varieties of Temperament*.

2. John B. Cortes, Florence M. Gatti, "Physique and Self-Description of Temperament," Journal of Consulting Psychology, 1965, Vol. 29, No. 5, p. 432-439.

Chapter 2

C. G. Jung's
Psychological Types

Psychological types are not the same as temperament types. They describe the different ways in which people perceive the world around and within them and make judgements about it.

Who was Dr. C. G. Jung?

C. G. Jung, 1875-1961, was a Swiss psychiatrist and psychologist. He was an early collaborator of Freud, a prolific writer whose collected works fill 18 volumes and the founder of a distinctive school of psychological thought that is being continued and developed until this day by a world-wide network of Jungian analysts and sympathizers.

Beyond these externals, Jung was an intrepid explorer of the inner world of the psyche. For him this inner world, which he called the unconscious, was not simply a basement filled with forgotten memories and useless junk, but was like an ocean or forest filled with beauty and danger, life and death, and meaningful discovery. It was out of his confrontation with the unconscious, both in himself and in his patients, that he slowly elaborated his psychology. His book *Psychological Types* acted as a compass or surveying tool by which he tried to understand his break with Freud, but more importantly, could begin to chart this world within.

The Basic Elements

Our first step in understanding Jung's types is to take a quick look at its basic elements. This is more to familiarize us with the terms used than to give us a deep insight into their meaning. Hopefully our understanding will deepen as we look at descriptions and examples of the 8 basic types.

18

The first two elements are extraversion and introversion. These words have entered into common English usage and many people are unaware that Jung brought this about and gave them precise meanings.

The extravert is someone whose energy and attention is directed outward to the people and things in the world around him, and those objects are decisive in the adaptation he makes and the actions he takes. For the extravert, the world around him is the real world and he adapts himself to it. His own inner world is less real to him and a secondary influence on his conduct.

In contrast, the introvert's energy and attention are directed inwardly. His own inner world is the real world which he adapts himself to and which determines his behavior. He strives to protect this inner world from too strong an influence from the outer world. This outer world is less real for him and therefore of less influence than the inner world.

Extraversion and introversion form a pair of opposite basic attitudes to life. Each of us is both extraverted and introverted, for we relate both to the world around us and the world within, but we tend to favor one attitude over the other.

In addition to the two basic attitudes there are 4 functions which are the ways in which the psyche makes contact with either the inner or outer world. These Jung called thinking, feeling, sensation and intuition.

He paired sensation and intuition together as two opposite ways of perceiving. Sensation is the perception of the immediate and tangible reality around us by way of seeing, hearing, touching, etc., and as such is familiar to us. Intuition is also a perception, but of what is in the background, i.e., hidden possibilities and implications. It is similar to the way we understand inspirations and hunches. We perceive something but we are not aware of how we got to that perception.

Thinking and feeling go together as a pair of opposite ways of making judgments. Thinking is the way of judging about the nature of things by means of our ideas and their organization. It concerns itself with the question of truth or falsity. It is not to be confused with intelligence. Feeling is an equivocal word in English. It can mean instincts, emotions and hunches as well. For Jung, its meaning is limited to a sense of rapport or lack of it by which we decide whether we like or dislike something, feel it is good or bad. It is not to be confused with having emotion.

Jung summarized the 4 functions like this:

"Sensations (i.e., sense perception) tells you that something exists; thinking tells you what it is; feeling tells you whether it is agreeable or not; and intuition tells you whence it comes and where it is going."

The Structure Common to Each Type

The attitude we use most can be called the dominant attitude, and the function we use most can be called the 1st function. For example, in the case of the extraverted sensation type, extraversion is the dominant attitude and sensation is the 1st function. Neither one stands alone. We do not find either simple extraverts, or sensation types without reference to introversion or extraversion. The function is always joined to the attitude.

The auxiliary function is the one which, instead of seeking its own goals, subordinates itself to the 1st function and aids it in its work. For example, the extraverted sensation type (ES) can have either thinking or feeling as an auxiliary function, and be an EST or an ESF. Let us call the auxiliary function the 2nd function.

The 3rd function also aids the 1st function, but it is usually less developed and less useful from the point of view of being consciously and freely used. The EST would have a 3rd function of feeling, while the ESF would have a 3rd function of thinking.

The last function, or least developed function, or inferior or 4th function is the one that is most opposite to the 1st function, and therefore tends to be the farthest away from consciousness because of its incompatability with the 1st function.

Just as the 1st function is always connected with an attitude, i.e., either introversion or extraversion, the other functions are as well. The 2nd function will share the attitude of the 1st to the degree that it is helping it. For example, the thinking of the EST will be extraverted. The 3rd function also shares the attitude of the 1st to the degree it is helping it, but usually it is of less help than the 2nd function because it is further from consciousness and therefore less developed. In many cases it shares the attitude of the 1st function with part of itself and the opposite attitude with another part of itself. For example, the feeling of the EST is often partially extraverted and useful to the EST part of the personality, yet part of it is introverted and less accessible and useful, but nonetheless valuable as we shall see.

The 4th function has an attitude opposite to that of the 1st function. In the ES, the 4th function is intuition (U) and its attitude is introverted.

We all possess both attitudes and all 4 functions, but they are arranged differently and it is these different basic arrangements that give rise to psychological types. How many basic psychological types are there? There are 2 possible conscious attitudes, 4 possible 1st functions and 2 possible 2nd functions, making 2x4x2 or 16 basic types. Our descriptions, however, will be based principally on 8 psychological types without always taking into account the difference in the 2nd function as for example, the difference between the ESF and the EST. This will make the descriptions less complicated, but the difference in the 2nd function is of practical importance when it is a question of the development of each type.

A Description of the Eight Psychological Types

Any description or example of one of the types tends to be misleading. This is because the description is one-sided in order to get the point across, while, as we have seen, we all contain both attitudes and all 4 functions. The best way to take the descriptions and stories that follow is as a jumping-off point for your own reflections and examples. See if someone you know embodies the characteristic traits of one of these types. Then you will have a living example and some personal practical verification of the validity of Jung's typology.

A Capsule Summary of the Eight Types

There are 4 extraverted types: the extraverted sensation type (ES), the extraverted intuition type (EU), the extraverted thinking type (ET), and the extraverted feeling type (EF). And there are 4 introverted types: the introverted sensation type (IS), the introverted intuition type (IU), the introverted thinking type (IT) and the introverted feeling type (IF). Each type hears his own particular kind of music.

The ES type loves to see, hear, taste, touch and smell the world around him or her.

The EU type is continually searching out new possibilities in the world around him or her.

The ET type has a plan he or she tries to carry out.

The EF type wants to be in harmony with the world around him or her.

The IS type is captivated by the vibrations that the outside world of the senses set off in him or her.

The IU type is continually searching out new possibilities in the world within him or her.

The IT type creates worlds of ideas in his or her mind.

The IF type dives deep into the pool of her or his own feelings.

The Extraverted Sensation Type

The extraverted sensation types (ES) are oriented outward to the world around them to the degree that it can be sensed. They are attuned to nuances of color and sound, as well as kinds and varieties of shapes, tastes, textures and the number and placement of objects. Their attention and energy goes forth and finds its sense of reality and satisfaction in all these tangible qualities of the physical world. They experience the sense object in all its vibrant life and detail. When the ES eats she pays attention to what she is eating and how it tastes and how she feels when she has eaten it. When she gets dressed she knows what colors she is putting on and how well-cared for her clothes are. When she enters a room she notices how many people are present and what the furnishings are like. For the young, healthy ES, whether man or woman, life is a festival of sensations which they enjoy.

> The usually bored and sullen crew of workers sat enthralled, their girlie magazines forgotten on their laps, watching Pete tell about his night on the town. His eyes gleamed, his white teeth flashed, his dark hair kept falling into his eyes, his arms would suddenly fling out while he told his story, and he paced up and down. Soon every man there felt his hands clench around the steering wheel of Pete's flashy white Cadillac, heard the music blaring in his ears, felt the beautiful girlfriend close beside him, her perfume wafting across his nose, and his foot pressing down on the gas pedal as the speedometer kept going up and up, their bodies swaying as they took the curves.

Either thinking or feeling can provide the ES type with a way of evaluating and making use of their sensations. ESs can be good cooks and house-builders, photographers, craftsmen, and business people. They see what is happening in a tangible, practical way and stick to the actual job to see that it gets finished. They even can have a Zorba-like exultation in being alive on this beautiful earth.

The ES who does not make enough use of his 2nd and 3rd functions can overuse his 1st. Then he tries to sense too much and too many things and not reflect on what these sensations mean but simply try to go on to new and more intense sensations. He can overeat or overaccumulate or overwork or simply overdo whatever his particular sense preference is. The people and objects around him begin to be treated as occasions or pretexts for more sensation, and he is so caught up in his sensing that he neglects his inner self.

> Dropping in for a little visit with Rich and Nancy set in motion a whole social ritual. Their friends would have been content to just sit there and talk, but Nancy insisted that they had to have a little snack. First came a tray of hot hors d'oeuvres, and then they both involved themselves in an elaborate process of making pizza pies. Then came the attentive eating of these beautiful creations. It was all delicious, but a bit too much, especially for Rich and Nancy who were always trying to diet.

Even when the 2nd and 3rd functions are being used, there comes a point where this kind of adaptation to life is not fully adequate because the inner self is not getting enough attention. This inner self is best represented by the 4th function of introverted intuition (IU) which is the way in which the ES can ask the question, "What is the meaning and purpose of my life?", "Where did I come from and where am I headed when I die?" This kind of questioning tends to be excluded from consciousness because it is too opposed to the 1st function and its extraverted attitude. Yet it is important because it represents another part of who the ES actually is. If the ES cannot consciously come to terms with this part of himself and tries to ignore it or bury it under a crowd of new sensations, then the IU dimension will begin to make itself felt, but in a negative and primitive way. The ES can become prey to negative intuitions of future disasters like planes crashing, or conspiracies being hatched.

Salvador was a master mason who built a good business on careful and precise work. He had gone to trade school and never had shown an interest in intellectual things. His family was surprised when they saw him reading books, and they became dismayed when they found that they all dealt with life on other planets and communication with space aliens. Sal didn't keep his knowledge to himself. With the zeal of a convert to a new faith he began telling everyone about them. He lived in two worlds. In the first he was a kind, open-hearted family man, and in the second he was one of the few who knew the inside story of flying saucers and government suppression and messages from beyond.

The Extraverted Intuition Type

The EU type's energy flows outward not to the external object but around it and through it to the possibilities it suggests. This type does not stop at the object of sensation like the ES type, but uses it as a spring-board to fly towards what could be. The EUs sparkle with new ideas and plans, many of which have real possibility and merit, for they are invested with the prime energies of the personality. They are prolific creators of new businesses, new machines, new social positions and organizations. For the young, healthy EU, life is an ever-changing drama with new adventures around every corner.

Mike's eyes danced with enthusiasm as he showed us a piece of land he had managed to buy in the country. Nobody else had even been able to find the land, but Mike had assembled the old maps and searched through the brush to find the old surveying markers. "I'm going to build a house here." He pointed to where a pile of salvaged lumber was stacked. "My well is half dug. It will be wonderful to live back here in the country away from the noise and smell of the city."

Either thinking or feeling can provide the EU type with a way of evaluating his intuitions. For example, the EUT not only gets the idea for a new business but uses his thinking function to plan out the necessary steps for its establishment, while the EUF not only sees the possibility of a new social service organization but can bring her feeling function to bear to encourage people to work with her in its establishment.

The EU who fails to develop his 2nd and 3rd functions gets caught up in more and more intuitions. They conceive one plan and expend enormous amounts of energy establishing it, but just as the goal gets within reach, they abandon it and leap head-long into a new adventure. They start one new project after another, oblivious to the reason for the failure of the previous one. They are always sowing new seeds but hardly ever reaping any of the harvest.

> "When are you going to move out to the new place?" we asked Mike when we saw him again. He looked away sheepishly and confessed that he had already sold his house in town and had cleared plenty of money, but instead of using it to work on the place in the country, somehow he had ended up buying a huge abandoned school house. Then, in spite of himself, he started getting excited again, telling us how he could build a home in front of the school house and then have storage in the back for all his junk cars until he got them fixed, and have a place to build animal pens, and . . .

Even when the auxiliary functions are being used, the EU is not completely adapted because his attention is still focused on the outer possibilities and not the needs of his inner self. He has to stop and ask the question, "Is the energy and time that is being spent on this intuition worth it to me personally in terms of my own needs and health and family life and social obligations?" Questions of this sort are hard for the EU to ask because it means pausing in the midst of his headlong rush after new possibilities.

The area that is least conscious for the EU is introverted sensation. It is very difficult for him to pay careful and meticulous attention to each detail that goes into the actual execution of his intuition, and it is even more difficult for him to let these sensations slowly soak into him and let himself perceive their implications. For example, he will not stop and listen to the sense impressions of his own body. Rather, he wears it down on his race after new intuitions. Because this area of IS is neglected, it begins to assail him as if from without in the form of physical accidents and sickness.

"What was it this time?", the guys at the shop asked Joe when he came in with his hand bandaged. Joe was always getting cut, bumped or bruised. This time he had tried to clean the sawdust from the top of the table saw while it was still running and had nicked himself. It was not quite as bad as when he had jacked up his car, pulled off a wheel and slid under for a look without taking the time to put in the jack stands. The car had almost landed on his head.

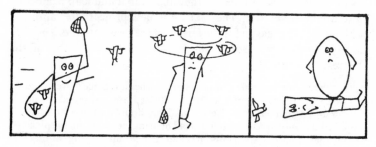

The Extraverted Feeling Type

The EF type wants to be in accord with the world around her. Her feeling rapport with the persons or objects in her environment is her most important driving force. She oils the troubled waters of society and is at the center of its social life. She tends to have many friends of all different sorts who come to bask in her flow of feeling and sympathy and go away glad that someone cares about them. Since the EF wants to be in rapport with the people around her, she takes her values from them as well. She wears the right clothes and has the right kind of spouse depending on the social circles she is living in.

Everybody loved Judy. There was always somebody leaning on her desk, or calling her on the phone. Even the clients who could barely tolerate some of the other workers loved to see her breezing down the hallway with a big smile on her face. She had a knack of focusing her interest on other people's problems and interests and they opened up like flowers under the bright sunshine. She joked and cajoled people into getting along, and at the office party she really came into her own.

The 2nd and 3rd functions of either sensation or intuition aid the EF in the accomplishment of this feeling rapport. For example, an EFS can make an excellent nurse, or teacher, for she develops a strong relationship to the patient or student and has the ability through the 2nd function to tend to their immediate needs. On the other hand, the EFU can be a good social worker who has a rapport with her clients and uses her intuition to discover what their real needs are.

When the EF either has not developed the auxiliary functions or has developed them and reached a state in life where a new kind of adaptation is needed, she can over-use her 1st function. She can exhaust herself in a whirl of visits, phone calls, shopping trips, and parties, and get so caught up in the succeeding objects of sympathy that she has no time to consider what her own personal opinions and judgments are. She can carry out extensive opinion polls among her many and varied friends as a substitute for making up her own mind.

A fuller adaptation to reality demands the ability to answer the question, "What do I really think?" The greatest weakness of the EF is introverted thinking, and it is this 4th function that holds the answer to the question of what her personal philosophy of life is. If she ignores this dimension of her personality it does not simply disappear, but it begins to afflict her in the form of negative thoughts about what other people are thinking about her. This begins to effect her rapport with the people around her and she makes social blunders that are inexplicable in terms of her 1st function.

> Pat had countless friends and it seemed that someone was always calling her up or dropping in to see her. She had the kind of warmth people made an effort to seek out, but sometimes she turned around and did something totally out of character. She might get an inconsequential phone call, and though she knew people were waiting to talk with her, she would let it drag on and on while they fumed, or suddenly she would snap at one of her friends. She felt she was getting worn out and overburdened with so many demands on her time, and once in a while something just slipped out.

In order to solve the problem of introverted thinking the EF can adopt ready-made philosophies and treat them like her own personal inventions.

When Joyce discovered Yoga she couldn't talk to anyone without trying to convert them. She didn't ask first what they believed to see whether they agreed with her or not, but she just assumed that what was new and wonderful to her would be new to everyone else and wonderful as well. Her friends were good-natured about it in the beginning, but after a while they began to resent her preaching.

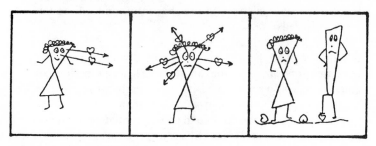

The Extraverted Thinking Type

For the extraverted thinker (ET), the plan he has thought up or has attached himself to is all-important in determining his behavior. For his plan he draws on the ideas and facts that exist in the world around him and he tries to execute his plan in the outer world. He can be very efficient in carrying out long and difficult operations which have to do with its accomplishment. For the ET the help of the 2nd or 3rd functions (sensation or intuition) gives him the ability to realize what he has thought up. If the 2nd function is sensation, for example, he will have a practical ability to execute his plan here and now. He can be a good mechanic or engineer or executive in charge of day-to-day operations. If intuition is the 2nd function he can be adept at finding innovative ways to carry out his conception.

Richard looked around his homestead. There was a road to build, land to clear, logs to haul, just lots of heavy work everywhere he looked. Suddenly the solution clicked. What he needed most of all was a bulldozer. The problem was money. Even a used one was well beyond his budget. But Richard wasn't going to let money stop him. He had a scrap pile of old car and truck parts, and he could always trade for more. Piece by piece he began to build his bulldozer, matching old transmissions and welding the various parts together. At the end, to the astonishment of everyone but himself, it ran and did the job.

28

The ET without the aid of the auxiliary functions, or even with their help, reaches a point where his adaptation to reality is too one-sided. He concentrates too intensely on his plans and they act like narrow formulas that squeeze the life out of everything around him and inside him as well. He becomes dogmatic and domineering. Whatever agrees or aids his plan is good, while whatever impedes it is evil.

The ET can become harsh and driven, and neglect his inner self. It is in the area of IF that this neglect is most severe. The ET has no time to answer the question, "How do I really feel about myself?" He neglects his health or finances, or personal life, in order to try to accomplish his plan, but the introverted feelings will not disappear. They turn on him and try to force their attention upon him in a negative way. His plans which were originally so objective and rational become filled with a secret self-seeking, and he acts hurt and resentful if someone does not agree with him.

When Cy would show up, his neighbors always had the uneasy feeling that it wasn't just to pass the time of day, but that he had some deal on his mind, and in this deal there was going to be a clear-cut winner, old Cy himself, and some sucker would be taken for a ride. After a while, sure enough, out it would come. "How about a wonderful truck (who knew how many miles the old wreck had on it?) for about 5 scrubby acres going to waste over in the back meadow?" (The best of the wood lot.)

The Introverted Types

The introverted types are more difficult to describe than the extraverted. Extraverts are out in broad daylight doing what they do in plain sight of everyone. But the flow of energy of the introvert is inward so their positive qualities are hidden. The extravert measures himself by and adapts himself to the external world we are all familiar with. The introvert is drawn by another world, the world within, and strives to discover and adapt himself to it. This inner world should not be understood as simply the ego, and thus the introvert as egocentric. The ego is but one dimension of the interior world which has a non-ego dimension which Jung called the collective unconscious. The inner world is the world of psychic images, dreams, myths and religious feelings which has its own reality.

Our Western civilization is at this point in time more extraverted than introverted in its stance. Introverts are looked upon as flawed extraverts who are not out-going enough. This bias makes it still harder for introverts to be understood not only by extraverts but by themselves. They can literally be prejudiced against their own attitude, having imbibed an extraverted stance from their environment. If we cannot accept the reality of an inner world, the whole spectrum of introverts will become inexplicable, for they will be seen as simply shunning the object and embracing mere subjectivity, which is a morass of self-centered musings and narcissistic preoccupations. The world within man is as real as the world without, no matter how difficult it might be to describe it.

The Introverted Sensation Type

The introverted sensation type (IS) is captivated not by the sense object but by the subjective sense impressions that this object awakens in him. The reverberations and repercussions of the object on his inner world are what his attention focuses on. It is as if a pebble has been thrown into a pond and the ripples spread out throughout the whole inner world of subjectivity, revealing not so much the qualities of the pebble but those of the water it has been thrown into. The sense impressions of the IS type have a different quality. They are not matter-of-fact like those of the ES type, but have overtones of myth and fantasy and deeper subjective values.

The 2nd and 3rd functions of thinking and feeling help organize and evaluate these impressions, but this process of organization goes on inside rather than outside. The IS has more trouble than his counterpart the ES in dealing with people and expressing himself. These things take a certain amount of extraversion and so come harder to the IS. The IS has to swim out of the depths, so to speak, to respond to the person who has caused the sense impressions within him. This can show itself in the form of slowness of speech or emotional response. The work of the IS is often meticulous and of the highest standards of craftsmanship, but it is done by a great expenditure of time and effort because of the distance that must be covered by them in order to create the exterior effect.

When the building inspector arrived at the site where Carl was building his house to do a preliminary inspection of the foundation, he couldn't quite believe his eyes. He had seen enough of home builders that nothing would have surprised him, except seeing concrete piers so perfectly true and carefully poured and finished that it excelled the work done by professional contractors. Little did he realize that years were going to pass before he had to come back for final inspection because each board and each sheet of sheetrock was going to be put in its place and carefully finished.

The very images that the IS perceives are difficult to communicate unless they have some kind of artistic gift by which to express the glow and mood that surrounds the sense object. The IS has to make a continual effort to express himself and not be caught up in his interior world of impressions and isolated from the everyday outer world.

Robert had noticed his cousins drive up to visit him from where he stood working on the porch steps, but he just stood and watched them park and come towards him. His gaze kept being pulled back to the step he was working on and to his tools which were neatly lined up. He had carefully measured the new pieces and now he would cut them and then...His cousins were puzzled by how aloof he seemed after they had gone out of their way to see him.

This type excels where attention to detail and order is important, whether it is the repair of delicate machines, the mastering of complicated inventories, or an especially intricate quilt of many pieces, sewn and embroidered with infinite care. The area most removed from the IS and therefore the weakest is that of the EU. However, good adaptation sometimes demands that we use this function. The IS tends to view EU as a disruption in his well-ordered life, but sometimes he has to face the question of a new job or a new place to live or a new business to establish. When the IS neglects his EU side he becomes prey to fears about future disasters. He feels anxieties that something is going to go wrong in the future despite his very careful ordering of the present.

> Betty couldn't stop worrying about Bob's job. He was the manager of the office and held the whole operation together. He had been there for years but still she worried. What if the company were taken over and Bob was fired, and then they lost the house and had to leave town and the kids would have to go to another school and . . .

The Introverted Intuition Type

The IU type gazes inward, not to the ripples of sensation caused by the object, but beyond these palpable facts to try to see their root and meaning. They are visionaries par excellence, seers and dreamers. They are caught up in explorations of the inner world and the possibilities of inner transformation. They can follow these inner paths by way of images and ideas, but they are always attempting to go deeper and find the ultimate origin and goal of the inner self.

> It hadn't been a typical date. She was surprised that Peter had even gotten around to asking her out at all. Now she sat in the restaurant gazing at him, for it was the first time she had ever really heard him talk about himself and what he was trying to do. He had been wandering with just a few dollars in his pocket around the country for almost a year, meditating in different spots, and he evoked the strange beauty and excitement of adventures in this inner world.

The 2nd and 3rd functions of thinking and feeling aid them in evaluating and organizing these inner journeys. The IU, without the aid of the auxiliary functions, wanders in a world of inner images or ideas, but never draws any implications from them as far as seeing how they should shape his own conduct. Even when the 2nd and 3rd functions are developed, the IU has difficulty in expressing his interior world because this demands a certain degree of extraversion. His words tend to be fragmentary and evocative, as if he cannot tear his eyes off his inner world long enough to formulate what is happening in everyday language. These attempts at expression are important, for without them the IU tends to become isolated and lose contact with ordinary realities.

> Michael sat at his desk, which was littered with books and papers, and scrawled on a tablet in barely legible writing. He was deeply immersed in his latest theories of subatomic particles. He was shocked out of his reverie when his wife told him to get dressed, for they were already late for their dinner engagement.

The greatest weakness of this type is in the area of ES. The IU finds it difficult to pay attention to the actual here-and-now physical world in which he lives. He inadvertently tends to bump into things, spill things, drop things, have his mind on something other than his food when he eats, and scarcely notices the clothes he wears or the colors of the walls of the rooms in which he lives.

> The professor bustled into the classroom late, as usual, sat down in the circle of chairs and placed his huge briefcase in front of him. His suit was rumpled and as he got up to search for his pipe, he managed to trip over the briefcase he had just put down. Tobacco began to dribble down his shirt as he waved the pipe in the air while he expounded on the subject of the day. Soon the pipe was forgotten, resting precariously on his knee, from there to slide into the already bulging briefcase. Too bad it hadn't been lit, for it was clear that a fire was the only way the briefcase would ever get cleared out. The students continued to watch, fascinated, as he punctuated his lecture by squirming around in his chair, slowly managing to dislodge his wallet from his pants pocket.

If the IU neglects this basic form of adaptation to reality, he is not simply excused from it. He becomes subject to obsessions and compulsions about sense objects, like sex or food, which are attempts by the ES part of the personality to capture his attention.

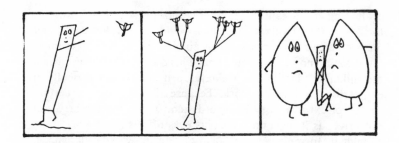

The Introverted Feeling Type

The IF tries to be in rapport with her inner world, whether it be of psychic images or ethical and spiritual values, and she tries to intensify this inner accord and embrace this world more deeply and fully. This is in sharp contrast with the EF, for with the IF the people and things around her are occasions of her feelings, which flow inward and go deeper and try to become more intense and concentrated.

> Joan moved contentedly about the school kitchen, preparing another good dinner for the children. She was a quiet and shy woman, who never said much but gave the feeling she liked her work, and when some of the kids would go out of their way to lend a hand, she would overcome her shyness and look directly at them with a glance overflowing with affection. That simple kind of thank-you was ample payment for the extra work they did.

Because of the direction of her feelings, the IF is often accused of not having any. She tries to protect herself against too strong an influence coming from the outer object and detach her feelings from it so that they can travel within. Her clinging to inner values, silent as it is, can provide a good example from an ethical and moral point of view. People around her sometimes sense this inner reality, and fidelity to inner values. But at other times they sense how they are somehow being treated with a certain reserve and held in check and subtly devalued.

The auxiliary sensing or intuition of the IF can help her perceive better the inner values she wants to adhere to, but this accentuation of the conscious function does not resolve the problem of expression that all the introverted types face. It is by the 3rd function, with its more extraverted side, that she often comes to grips with the outside world around her. The IFs can be literally bursting with feelings but have no ready way to communicate them both because of their direction and because their content is not readily explicable in everyday terms. Sometimes the feelings will make themselves felt in some sort of artistic production or act of charity.

This problem of expression is bound up with their relationship to the outer world. It is by extraverted sensing or intuition that they can begin to perceive what the outer world is like, but the most difficult thing for them to do is to develop their extraverted thinking.

> Nancy picked up the letter from her friend again. It had been four months since she had promised to send the packages to her. They had been left ready and waiting, and all that had to be done was to bring them to the post office, but somehow she just couldn't get around to it. The night before she had had a nightmare about it. She should go down right now and mail them off, but she continued to procrastinate.

If the IF cannot tackle a task consciously it can happen to her in an unconscious manner. Then she begins to feel that other people are thinking negative and dangerous things about her, and she has to fight these plots against her with counterplots.

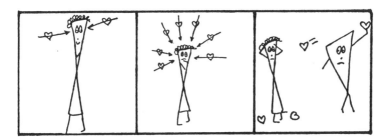

The Introverted Thinking Type

While the ET starts from external facts and ideas and ends up with plans to be accomplished, the IT is not oriented to outer facts, though he might make some use of them, but wants to explore the nature and structure of his inner world of ideas. His thinking tends to be more intenseve than extensive, as if he wants to embrace the whole world with one thought.

> Ken was quiet and self-contained, but with a muted driving sharpness of mind. No one took advantage of his quiet nature, and when his friends had a problem, they sought his advice. Harriet, for example, was buying a new swimming pool, and fearful of making the decisions herself, invited Ken to go with her to the dealer. Once there he didn't say a word until after the selection had been made and the papers were just about to be signed. Then he quickly stepped in and drove a hard bargain that saved her almost $1,000.

The 2nd and 3rd functions of sensing and intuition help him develop this interior world of thought. If intuition dominates, he may have the inclination to think about philosophy or law or theoretical science. If sensation dominates, he may be attracted to business or accounting or applied science. The IT shares a difficulty in expressing his inner world with the rest of the introverts. Often his expressions do not fully convey the rich life within. But expression is important as a link to the outer everyday world.

The greatest weakness of the IT is in the area of EF, which is the way by which we have rapport with the people around us, sympathize with them and are sympathized with in return.

> When Larry arrived at the new office he saw right off things had been sliding. There were a lot of welfare cases where grounds existed for disqualification. Take old Peterson, for example. Here it was in black and white that his burial policy was worth $100, while it clearly stated in the manual that $50 was the maximum allowable value. Case Disqualified.

The IT without EF tends to become isolated in our society. If he cannot make contact with his EF, it falls upon him in the form of excessive touchiness and readiness to take offense. He can become bigoted, argumentative, and accuse others of not caring for him. This negative feeling can even fasten itself to his conscious world of thought and begin subtly to distort its objective and rational character. Then he tries to use his profession or thinking function to justify his feelings. His objectivity becomes a kind of cunning.

Old Sam looked like a fat friendly farmer until you asked a favor of him or watched his cold icy-blue eyes when he was planning one of his deals. There was the time, for instance, when he got Ned to put up a new barn in exchange for one of his old tractors. Somehow, even though Ned was a shrewd character himself, Sam ended up with a practically complete barn and the tractor.

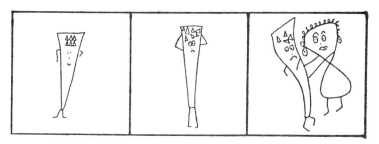

What is Your Psychological Type?

We have one great advantage when it comes to discovering our own psychological type in contrast to someone else's. We have a tremendous amount of material in the form of past memories and present attractions and conflicts that we can draw on to see if there is an underlying pattern of behavior. Unfortunately, this very wealth of material and our easy access to it can sometimes complicate our estimation of our own type. We remember not only the things we have done with our conscious personality but the feelings, thoughts, insights and impressions that come from all aspects of ourselves. Sometimes it takes a while to sort out this material.

When it comes to recognizing other people's type there is no simple rule or method we can use in order to arrive at an infallible conclusion. Sometimes our first impressions are very accurate and are confirmed by later intimate knowledge. At other times even extensive contact with another person leaves us puzzled and without any certain knowledge as to their type.

The place to start with our actual recognition of types is with our own. The more intimately we understand our own type the better we can move from this knowledge to an objective knowledge of someone else's type. What is your own type? Did one of the 8 descriptions come close enough so that you have a fair degree of certainty? Try to decide whether you are introverted or extraverted. Which is your more habitual or ordinary way of proceeding? Next try to decide whether your thinking function or your feeling function is more dominant. As a general rule of thumb the feeling function in women is usually more dominant than their thinking function, and the thinking function in men is usually more dominant than their feeling function. It is not usual to find men with a 1st function of feeling or women with a 1st function of thinking, nor is it particularly common to find men with a 2nd function of feeling and women with a 2nd function of thinking. Sensation and intuition appear less related to sex differences. Again, remember that the position of the thinking function has nothing to do with intelligence.

Next try to decide whether sensation or intuition is more dominant. Once you have chosen the dominant functions from the thinking-feeling pair and the sensation-intuition pair, compare the two in order to decide which function is first. As an aid for this kind of selection, do the self-discovery quizzes and see which elements you favor.

Put a check next to the item that best represents your normal and habitual way of doing things. Sometimes it is helpful to imagine ourselves answering these questions as if we are a young person of 18 or 20 because this brings out our innate attitude better at times than answering out of a later stage of development. If there are some questions where neither alternative seems to fit, just ignore the question and go on.

Self Discovery Quiz for Introversion and Extraversion

	Introversion	Extraversion
I like being around people	_only sometimes	_almost always
For get-togethers I usually favor	_small groups	_large groups
People would call me	_quiet and reserved	_outgoing
I compliment people	_only sometimes	_often

Continue on p. 39

Self-Discovery Quiz for Introversion and Extraversion (Continues)

	Introversion	Extraversion
People would call me	_reflective	_active
I like to have casual visitors	_once in a while	_often
I find the idea of spending a few days in bed	_interesting	_boring
People would say I am	_hard to get to know well	_easy to know
In a gathering I am inclined to	_find someone to talk to	_join in the group conversation
When speaking to strangers I	_sometimes hesitate	_find it quite easy
At parties I	_rarely find it interesting	_usually have a good time
In meeting new people I make the first move	_occasionally	_most of the time
When it comes to saving money I find it	_not too difficult	_a real chore
When I hear the telephone I	_recoil a little	_get a good feeling of anticipation
When it is a question of some-one else's plans I am inclined to	_bow out	_join in
When I am in a new group I tend more to	_listen	_talk
The number of close friends I have is	_a few	_quite a few

Self-Discovery Quiz for Thinking and Feeling

	Feeling	Thinking
I am more impressed by	_emotions	_principles
People would consider me	_warm and sympathetic	_reasonable
When people argue I want them to	_stop	_come up with an answer
I am more inclined to devote myself to	_my friend's problems	_causes
I enjoy hearing sarcasm	_only rarely	_fairly often
When I have to make an important decision I	_trust my feelings	_try to reason it out

Continue on p. 40

39

Self-Discovery Quiz for Thinking and Feeling (Continues)

	Feeling	Thinking
I am more inclined to care about	_rapport	_logic
When something bad happens to one of my friends I	_sympathize	_look for an explanation
When watching a melodrama on T.V. I	_tend to cry	_criticize the plot

Self-Discovery Quiz for Intuition and Sensation

	Intuition	Sensation
I tend to	_get excited about future	_savor the present moment
When I have set plans	_I feel somewhat tied down	_I am comfortable with them
If I were to work for a manufacturer I would prefer	_research and design	_production and distribution
Orderliness	_isn't crucial	_really appeals to me
If people were to complain about me they would say	_I have my head in the clouds	_I am in a rut
When I sit down at my main meal I	_am happy enough to get it over with	_like to linger a bit and savor it
People would say I am more	_speculative	_realistic
I like	_frequent variety	_set patterns
When I come across a new situation I am more interested in	_what is possible	_what is actual
In doing ordinary things I tend to	_make up my own way	_do it the usual way
I like better to	_invent new plans	_carry out set plans
The mistake I am most inclined to is	_to get involved in so many things I can't finish them.	_not to start the new projects I want to do
People would call me more	_imaginative	_matter-of-fact

Try to come to a tentative conclusion as to what your psychological type is, including the 2nd function. Check this description to see if the 2nd and 3rd functions are opposites, as well as the 1st and 4th.

Sometimes determining what the 4th function is is helpful in psychological type diagnosis. The 4th function can be more obvious or more noticeable at times than the 1st. We can describe the 1st function as differentiated, positive, energetic, and controlled, while the 4th tends to be primitive, fascinating, frightening, and not fully controllable. What is your particular weakness? It should turn out to be the opposite of the 1st function.

1. Sensation as the 4th function shows itself in clumsiness, stumbling, dropping things, forgetting details, skinned knuckles, cut fingers, and a difficulty in sticking with routine jobs.

2. Intuition as the 4th function shows itself in fear of future disasters or illnesses or accidents.

3. Feeling in 4th place makes itself known in an inability to easily express the polite sentiments called for by various social situations, by occasionally dropping remarks that strike people the wrong way, and by sometimes being brusque with someone you really want to show affection to.

4. Thinking in the 4th place is shown in an inability to make decisions and orderly plans for the accomplishment of our personal affairs, and a tendency to substitute someone else's thinking or a ready-made system of thought for our own.

Notes on Further Study

The best source for a further study of psychological types is Jung's *Psychological Types*. In it he not only gives detailed descriptions of each type but even more importantly he makes it clear that a study of types has to do with a study of the whole personality, both conscious and unconscious. Marie Louise Von-Franz, one of Jung's closest collaborators, has a small book called *The Inferior Function* which is based on a series of lectures she gave at the C.G. Jung Institute in Zurich. This, too, is very instructive when trying to get a deeper understanding of the 4th function. The best source of information about Jung's life is *Memories, Dreams, Reflections* which concentrates on his inner experiences and how they gave birth to his psychological theories, and it makes fascinating reading.

Chapter 3

Putting the Body, Temperament and Psychological Type Together

Now that we have introduced body, temperament, and psychological types, we have to ask the question of whether or not they are related and can go together to form one typology. We will look at this question in some detail in Chapter 8, but the best way for you to answer it is not on theoretical grounds that say "they can't be", or "they must be", but by looking to your own experience. The more you can type people on all three levels starting with yourself, the more you will have the basic facts in hand to determine if there is a relationship between body, temperament and psychological types. Figuring out types is a skill, and simply reading type descriptions will not make you an expert in it. It takes time and energy and experience to develop and perfect this ability, but it is well worth the effort.

This is how we established the relationships that are described in this chapter: we typed people using both Sheldon and Jung, and gradually began to see a pattern. Even if this pattern were 100% correct, it will not do you any good unless you can see it yourself day-by-day in the people around you. Personal experience is the best kind of evidence.

Since we do not have friends in common and an opportunity to examine them together, let us look at Sheldon's description of the various temperaments to see if we can find some clues about what psychological type they belong to. Our first clue is in the fact that Sheldon called the ectotonic an introvert, while he felt both the endotonic and the mesotonic were extraverts, but of different kinds.

The Psychological Type of the Endotonic

The numbers in parentheses refer to traits in Sheldon's scale of temperament and the page number to his *Varieties of Temperament*.

The endotonic is an extravert. He loves to have people around, a trait Sheldon called sociophilia (8). He is dependent on them for affection and approval (10). The endotonic does not hold back his emotions; whatever is there flows readily and smoothly out (17) and can be easily understood. He wants to be around people when he is troubled (19). He is well-oriented to the social world around him and knows what the general opinion of the community is about many individuals in it (11).

The endotonic has sensation for his 1st function. He is oriented to the world around him through his sense impressions. *"Endotonics can always be trusted to maintain a close grip on immediate practical reality." (p. 249-250). "Endotonia means realism. Endotonic ecstasy lies in the achievement of a 'real' surrounding made up of nice things that taste good, smell good, look good, sound good, feel good." (p. 253).* He loves to eat (4) and to be physically comfortable (2), and he likes people simply because they are with him without making judgments about them (9). They are facts which he accepts (13).

The endotonic has intuition as his 4th function. He tends to lack foresight and a sense of progress. He is not a reformer (16). He views the ectotonic as a *"dark and suspicious person, a miser at best and a sinister influence at worse"* (p. 37) which is a good description of the negative intuition of the ES.

The Psychological Type of the Male Mesotonic

The mesotonic is an extravert, with relatively little grasp of his inner self (17). His is an extraversion of action. He loves physical adventure (2) and is full of energy to be doing things (3). He is physically courageous for combat (8) and has an unrestrained voice (13). He dislikes being enclosed in small places (11).

The 1st function of the mesotonic is thinking. The mesotonic knows what he wants and he has a *"singularly impersonal objectivity in seeking what is wanted"* (p.55). He is effective in carrying out decisions without inhibitions. He is stable, predictable, and hardheaded (p. 58). He gets things done without always stopping and considering the physical and social costs (p. 59). *"The even regulation of habitual overt behavior in mesotonics is striking, but it is perhaps relatively unimportant in comparison with the same habitual ordering of mental activities"* (p. 265). This habitual ordering of the mental activities is a result of the predominance of the thinking function.

The least developed function of the mesotonic is feeling. The negative side of the efficiency in getting things done is callousness towards people and things that get in their way (11). As Sheldon puts it, they have a *"singular insensitivity, especially to the less obvious or subtler needs or desires of other personalities in the environment"* (p. 57). On occasions the unconscious feeling suddenly reveals itself in the form of sudden conversion with religious overtones (p. 65) which represents the introverted feeling side of the personality.

The Psychological Type of the Ectotonic

The ectotonic is an introvert. *"The thing to be saved and protected at all costs is the continuity and the integrity of the inner awareness. Such a person disassociates the outer objective reality but remains in the closest touch with his own inward subjective reality."* (p. 88). The ectotonic loves privacy (4), tends to avoid much socializing (8) and is restrained both in voice (9) and in the expression of emotions (6).

The most developed function of the ectotonic is intuition. He has a great deal of curiosity and moves from one new interest to another. *"He seems to be able to change his mind abruptly and suddenly adapt all his feelings and attitudes to the new orientation."* (p. 82). He is oriented to the future (20) and wants to understand the riddles of life (p. 93). *"One of the most striking characteristics of persons showing the C-17 trait (introversion) predominantly is their acuity and preciseness of intuition. Intuition is of the first order in these people, for it is based on a thorough familiarity with the remote consciousness from which it springs."* (p. 89).

The least developed function is sensation. He cannot seem to accept physical realities matter-of-factly. He has difficulty in forming routines and habits (10) and difficulty in learning things by rote. He either ignores things or reads too much into them. *"Ectotonics desire but little, but they seem to become inordinately attached to what they have both in the sense of material goods and in the sense of personal loyalties."* (p. 37). Physical objects become alive to them. *"He becomes affectionately attached to things, reads human qualities and feelings into them and often focuses deep affection upon things that are not human."* (p. 255). He can have an especially difficult time dealing with sexuality. *"The ectotonic is always in danger of flying too far from the earth and suffering an Icarian fall"* (p.250).

The Type Tool Diagrams

Let us place the ES, the ET, and the IU on the diagram of somatotypes, Figure 2.

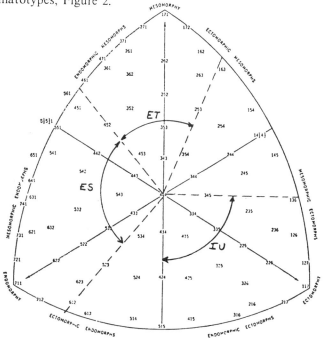

Fig. 2. Psychologocal Types of the Endomorph, Mesomorph and Ectomorph.

This leaves us with the question of where the other 5 psychological types are to be located. Unfortunately, Dr. Sheldon did not provide us with detailed descriptions of the mixed temperaments in which we could try to discover the other psychological types. Figure 3 represents our own estimates of where the other types fall for men.

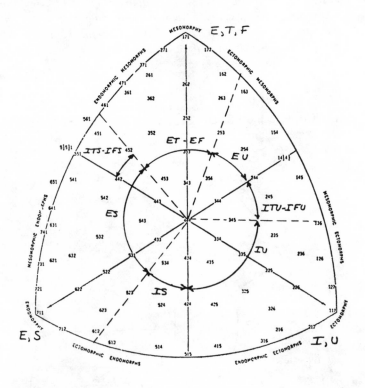

Fig. 3. Psychological Types of Male Somatotypes

Sheldon found that women tend to be less mesomorphic and more endomorphic than men. Figure 4 represents the divisions into psychological type for women where the center has been shifted away from the pole of mesomorphy and towards the pole of endomorphy. A woman who is an EF could have less mesomorphy than a man who is an ET.

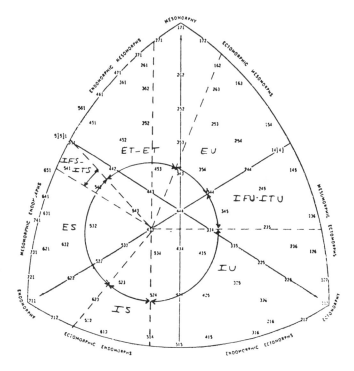

Fig. 4. Psychological Types of Female Somatotypes.

If we study Figure 3 there is a certain interior logic in it. Let us imagine that each of the three corners is like the pole of a three-pole magnet. Each pole has the strongest influence on the area that is closest to it and its power of attraction weakens with distance. Between the IU pole and the ET, EF pole we find first the ITU and the IFU and then the EU, while between the ET, EF pole and the ES pole we find the ITS and IFS. Between the IU and the ES poles we find the IS. The only strange placement is that of the ITS and the IFS which at first glance seems like it should be on the other side next to IU territory and together with the ITU and IFU.

The Type Tool diagrams should not be taken as finished products. A great deal more experience and experimentation must go on in order to determine exactly where the boundaries between types are and whether they overlap or not. Detailed body and temperament descriptions like those of Sheldon for the 3

47

polar extremes remain to be written based on extensive observations of the body and temperament corresponding to the other 5 basic psychological types. What follows are simply tentative notes on the body and temperament type of each psychological type.

The IU Type and ET Type and ES Type

We have already seen Sheldon's description of the body types and temperaments that correspond with the ES, ET and the IU. The thing to note is that while Sheldon was describing the extremes of each somatotype, the territory of each psychological type covers a wide area made up of many somatotypes and temperaments. We should not expect the IU to always resemble a bean pole or the ES to look like Santa Claus.

The IU covers a wide range of physiques from the walking stick to the slim muscularity of the mesomorphic ectomorph to the bulkiness of the endomorphic mesomorph and the midrange balanced body types. In the same way the temperament varies and no doubt the psychological type within the limits of the IU type.

The ES ranges from the roundness of the polar extreme to the burliness of the endormorphic mesomorph who might actually have more mesomorphy than endomorphy and he, too, shares in the midrange balanced somatotypes, who at first glance seem almost the same as the midrange physiques that belong to other psychological types.

The ET ranges from the extreme polar mesomorphs to the ETS who is heavy-set and chunky under the influence of the endomorphic pole and the ETU who is leaner but still heavily muscled, who is closer to the ectomorphic pole.

The Introverted Sensation Type

The Body Type

The physique of the IS is that of an endomorph-ectomorph, sometimes with little mesomorphy, but ranging up to the midrange body type. We should not think of the roundness of the endomorph as an opposite to ectomorphy. The IS has a roundness which is extended and spread out in space by ectomorphy. In this way he can be distinguished from the predominant endomorphy of the more extreme ES who is more spherical at the endomorphic pole and more muscular further north on the somatotype chart.

The Temperament Type

The IS shows a special type of ectotonic behavior due to his introverted sensation. He has a love of privacy and is restrained in voice and in the expression of his emotions. He does not have the easy extraversion of affect of his neighbor the ES. His emotions, while strong, are held in and shyly bestowed. He does not exhibit the quick friendliness, tolerance and indiscriminate amiability found in the ES. He can set a good table but does not make the same social sacrament out of eating.

The ectotonia of the IS takes on a different character because sensation replaces intuition. The IS is more orderly and meticulous with details and observant of routines. Their houses are often particularly neat and clean in marked contrast with the IU who sins by omission and inadvertence, and the ES who fails by lack of organization. They show none of the quick curiosity and reaction and movement from one topic to another characteristic of the ectotonic IU.

He shows little of the love of risk and chance and competition that is found in the mesotonic. He is by nature conservative and conserving. He tends to keep what he has and keep it well. When he accumulates money it is more from careful use than daring entrepreneurial acts.

The Extraverted Intuition Type
The Body Type

The physique of the EU is that of the ectomorphic mesomorph. His ectomorphy makes his muscles stand out in clean, sharp relief so that the degree of mesomorphy could tend to be overestimated at first glance. The EU often gives the impression of lean muscularity and speed. The 254 somatotype which Sheldon likens to an ocelot or cheetah falls in this range. Peterson in his *Atlas of*

Children remarks about one of his 254 boys, *"He loves freedom above all and does not want to be tied down to anything whatsoever. Seemingly his most profound need is to be independent."*

The Temperament Type

The EU shares the extraversion of action of the more mesotonic ET. There is a love of physical adventure and an enjoyment in being out and doing things. He is outgoing and physically courageous but without the same aggressiveness and love of domination that marks the more extreme mesotonic. Neither does he share the mesotonic's knack of rubbing people's feelings the wrong way. He is quick in movement and accident-prone, and his tolerance for pain is mixed with a certain amount of concern for his health. Instead of being youth-oriented he is future-oriented.

He shares the ectotonic's intuition, but not his introversion. He looks to the future outside, changes activities quickly and resists habit and routine. He chafes under authority and loves freedom and independence.

The EU forms a strong contrast with the endotonia of the ES. He is fast to react, slow to relax and unwilling to take time out to eat. While being warm and friendly among the people he knows well, he shows little of the tolerance and indiscriminate amiability of the ES.

The Extraverted Feeling Type

The Body Type

The range of the EF type covers much of the territory of the ET but with fewer people at the polar extremes and more in the midrange since most EFs appear to be women. The EF territory might also extend further south than the ET territory but have the same basic separation into the EFS and the EFU.

The Temperament Type

The EFs show the mesotonic extraversion of action and are

generally energetic and well-liked. But this is female mesotonia with feeling in the first place instead of thinking, and so the male mesotonic qualities like love of physical adventure, risk and chance and combative aggressiveness are all toned down. The EFs can be athletic, lively and assertive without being combative. The EF's muscles, while not as pronounced as the the male mesotonic's, make nicer curves and they have an effect physically in the high energy level and temperamentally in the ability of this type to control and dominate a situation with a combination of physical presence and focused feeling. People tend to want to do what they want them to do. Like the male mesotonic, the female looks with nostalgia on youth as the time of physical perfection. They tend to mature earlier and feel older earlier, and be concerned about their beauty fading.

The Introverted Thinking and Introverted Feeling Types

The Body Type

It appears that this type covers two distinct territories; one next to the IU, which has the ITU and the IFU, and another on the other side which contains the ITS and the IFS. Since this is the only instance where a type territory is split up there is a chance that we are mistaking a portly 444 ITS for a more endomorphic and/or mesomorphic physique which would place the ITS and IFS on the other side. It is striking, however, that all the types with sensation in the 1st or 2nd place fall on the left side of the diagram and the ITS and IFS fit into this pattern, so we will describe these types as living in two separate territories.

The physiques of the ITU and the IFU often, at first glance, look like the mesomorphic IUs. Some of these two types are long and thin, but with a closer examination they show a greater degree of wiry mesomorphy than the IUs. The ITS and the IFS appear to cover part of the same territory as the more mesomorphic ES.

The Temperament Type

The ITU and the IFU share many of the traits of the ectotonic

IU with whom they share their introversion and to a lesser degree their intuition, such as love of privacy, emotional restraint, as well as a reluctance to socialize. In a lesser degree they share the quick reactions of the more extreme ectotonics and what Sheldon calls mental over-intensity or hyperattentionality. The ITU, because of the placement of the thinking function, has what could be called an introverted or mental mesotonia in contrast to the more physically active mesotonia of the ET. He does not boom out vocally or try to dominate a social situation, but he has an inner hardheadedness and mental drive, and it can produce through the inferior feeling function a disregard and callousness or obliviousness to the feelings of others that mirrors in its own way the inferior feeling of the mesotonic.

The IFU differs from the ITU much like the ET differs from the EF. The traits due to introversion remain in place, like love of privacy, etc., but the character of the mesotonia changes to a more feminine one without the same ruthlessness that comes from feeling in the 4th place. The IFU can sometimes appear somewhat lifeless because the feelings are not immediately visible.

The ITS and the IFS can be mistaken at first glance for more or less amiable ESs. Despite appearances they possess little of the sociophilia and smooth extraversion of feeling that is the hallmark of the endotonic. They share with the rest of the ectotonics a certain distinctive self-conscious movement of the eyes. It is almost as if they are introverts in extraverted bodies.

The ITS can be a businessman with a difference. He has the mental equipment to pay attention to practical detail combined with the introvert's instinct for preservation. Add to this a love of competition and dominating and a dash of ruthlessness that comes from the mesotonia and it can be a formidable combination for material success.

The IFS will again differ in characteristic fashion with the ectotonic love of privacy, sociophobia, vocal restraint and secretness of feeling but without the sense of competition and domination found in the ITS.

What is Your Type?

The 444 somatotype appears divided among the 8 psychological types and relatively small changes in somatotype in the midrange physiques are associated with different psychological types. This must be kept in mind when evaluating someone's type. We have to avoid the tendency to oversimplify or stereotype by only associating the more extreme physiques with their corresponding psychological types.

The Type Tool is a knowledge of your body, temperament and psychological type, in short, your complete type, that expresses itself on these three levels. With it you will be able to start working on your self-development and your relationships with other people. Part II describes how to start on this process. Before you begin, assess the knowledge you have of your type, list what you think you are at each level and find your place on the Type Tool diagram. See if your estimations of body, temperament and psychological type fall in roughly the same area.

Part II
Develop Your Own Type

Chapter 4

Your Type
and its Development

Types Static and Dynamic, and Possibly Dangerous

The best possible result of working your way through Part I is the discovery of your own type. This discovery, though it is the end of one process, is just the beginning of another. The knowledge of one's own type is simply the key that opens the door to the adventure of typological development.

The fact that you are born a certain type does not detract in the least from the fact that from the moment of your conception you are being shaped and molded by the world around you. Types are dynamic. We have to develop within ourselves and we have to grow in our relationships with the world around us. This chapter concentrates on type development within, while the next looks at how we interact with our environment. The one thing types are not are labels we can pin on and forget about.

The study of types is not a parlor game. When taken seriously it is an important tool by which we can increase our inner well-being, but like a chisel or a chainsaw, it demands a certain amount of respect. There is nothing wrong with looking after our own psychic health, for it is our own responsibility, just like good nutrition is. But types open the door between the conscious and the unconscious, and when the door is open we cannot always close it at will. Therefore, if you suspect you have serious psychological problems, don't open this door without help available, in the form of a knowledgeable person who can lend a hand if things get rough.

Types are meant to help us with our real life problems whether it is of self-confidence or realizing our true potential or helping our marriage or finding a mate or getting along with the people around us. It is often hard work which is both tiring and humbling, and we do it because we see we have to if we want to get out of the deadend we are in and find a deeper and richer life.

The Development of the Body Type

One day our young and somewhat ectomorphic son showed us, with a wistful expression, a photo of a muscle-building ad in a popular magazine. It featured the usual 7 in mesomorphy and showed two sketches. The first showed an ectomorph being transformed into a mesomorph, while the 2nd showed an endomorph undergoing the same process. Unfortunately for the dreams of young boys, such transformations simply don't happen, nor do they happen for girls who are going to be changed into big-breasted, slim and long-legged beauties by diet or exercise programs, so every girl would look like a Hollywood starlet. Sheldon found that the basic body or somatotype remains unchanged during life despite weight gain or loss, and the state of physical conditioning. In what way, then, can we understand the development of the body type?

The body type shows the least change of the 3 levels of type, but even here there can be meaningful development centered on the removal of false hopes and the strategy of making the most of what we have.

Development and Endomorphy

Height and weight tabes, even when they are divided into light, medium and heavy frames, are often inadequate and misleading. Each body type has its own normal height-weight pattern through life. Sheldon in his *Atlas of Men* provides these patterns for 88 distinct somatotypes. It is discouraging for a person with a substantial degree of endomorphy to be constantly feeling guilty because they are overweight according to the usual height-weight tables. If they knew the real normal weight for their body type they would have a more reasonable goal to aim at. In the same way, mothers try to fatten up ectomorphic children who are supposedly underweight, and all they succeed in doing is worrying themselves and perhaps giving the child a momentary little pot-belly.

The first step in dealing with the endomorphy is to set realistic weight goals. These goals will be modified according to our degree of training or physical conditioning. Sheldon found that highly conditioned people were sometimes 10% below the norms for their body type. Differences in diet will make the weight norms vary from country to country, and even within the country. Diet is another area which must be regulated according to body type, not only according to the kind of food but the frequency. The digestive system varies in efficiency and capacity from somatotype to somatotype. Two people on the same diet react differently, with one getting fat and the other not showing any weight gain. Sleep needs also vary by body type, as well as the inclination to go to sleep, to get up, the number of hours of sleep we need, etc.

Development and Mesomorphy

Within the degree of mesomorphy we have we can be well-conditioned or ill, with our muscles in a hard or soft state. It is as pointless to set general exercise goals without first determining who it is that is exercising from the point of view of body type as it is to set weight goals. Indiscriminate athletic competition between people simply of the same age, or same height and weight, implies a view of a uniformity of bodies that flies in the fact of facts. Performance to be meaningful has to be related to who is performing and what their natural endowment is. To pretend that all have an equal chance of winning, which is dependent on how hard they are willing to work, is simply wrong and condemns the vast majority to be losers who have not tried hard enough. Within our own body type we can be in good condition and try to be better within these limitations. Then our goals are more realistic and more likely to lead to real progress.

Development and Ectomorphy

While weight and conditioning are easy enough to relate to endomorphy and mesomorphy, what can be said about ectomorphy which has to do with linearity, surface area and height? What we must look to is the nervous system associated with these traits. From this point of view ectomorphy, which functions like a receptive system, demands a measure of physical privacy in order to assimilate the signals received. The more ectomorphic the body is the more it has to shield itself from overstimulation so as not to overload the system with too many signals. However, to the degree that ectomorphy is lacking, there is a danger of being too social and action-oriented and not paying attention to these same signals due to their less intense reception. Then the risk is not to pay attention to the demands of the inner world which get lost in a whirl of activity. Ectomorphy in a developmental sense is a need for quiet and time for listening.

We must pay attention to the 3 basic components of our physique in order to avoid overtaxing the weaker ones and making the best use of the stronger ones. This problem is made more complicated when different areas of our own body vary in type. Sheldon called this dysplasia and found that in certain cases it could create serious problems. It shows itself in any number of ways, as, for example, in a boy with a normal masculine physique who has arms that more like a girl's so he can't throw or fight. Or the case of a girl who has hips that are larger than her chest and feels that it ruins her figure and her chance with boys. Or in a highly athletic physique where there is enough mesomorphy for top flight competition except for the fact that the legs are weaker than the rest of the body.

The recognition of these variations within the same body type can prevent a great deal of frustration. These kinds of things are what they are, and while their adverse impact can be minimized by working around the problem, they cannot simply be rooted out. The would-be athlete can train his legs to their maximum potential, but he has to realize this could very well not be enough for professional competition. The young lady with big hips can make sure she has no extra weight, and dress to look more slender, but the underlying bone structure will not go away. What is of the most importance is the avoidance of years of frustration in trying to do what we are not endowed to do when there are many gifts that each of us have that remain under-developed.

The Development of Temperament

It is easier to grasp the idea of development in the area of temperament, for while it is conditioned by our body type, it deals with our basic way of behaving. Still and all, our behavior does not exist in a vacuum so we can change it in any direction with equal ease. The discovery of our temperament type can give us an idea of what our particular strengths and weaknesses are. The greater strength we have in a component the more we tend to use it and over-use it while we try to ignore that area we are underendowed in, hoping it will go away. We can summarize the 3 basic elements of temperament as follows:

All Needed

Endotonia: A love of eating, comfort and people.
Mesotonia: A love of independent decision-making and action.
Ectotonia: A love of reflection.

Each component is necessary for an adequate adaptation to the ever-changing circumstances of our life. On the level of body type no one would suggest they could do without the digestive system or muscular system or nervous system. On the level of temperament type we have our needs as well which cannot be ignored, i.e., our need for people and decisive action and reflection. Each person will need his own particular combination, and in the sections on the the 8 psychological types and their development we will look at these different combinations more closely.

The Development of the Psychological Type

It is in the area of psychological type that the notion of development takes on its fullest meaning. Here we are the furthest removed from the biologically given fact of the body and closest to our inner selves who can know and choose. Yet even here it is not all liberty without structure. Our development takes place within the overall structure of our particular psychological type. We can develop the totality of ourselves which contains the two attitudes of introversion and extraversion, as well as the 4 functions, but our attainment of this wholeness follows a particular path for each type.

We have already seen in our description of the 8 psychological types how there seems to be a basic pattern. As you read the following sketch think of your own psychological type.

There is the 1st function with its attitude in the center of the stage and the spotlight on him; he is the star. The 2nd function is playing a supporting role and the 3rd might come on for a bit part. They all make up the conscious play under the spotlight of the ego. But where is the 3rd when he is not reciting his few lines? And more importantly, where is the 4th? He comes popping in, swinging on a rope whenever he has a mind to, no matter what the script says. And he spouts off crazy or wonderful, or stupid things and runs off. What are we going to do with that guy? He seems to be ruining the show. Why work so hard over the script only to have some idiot run out, not during rehearsals but at the most important performances, right in front of everyone. Our first inclination is to throttle him, give him a swift kick and lock him up backstage, but he is some kind of escape artist, so that doesn't work. Next we can try to just ignore him and really concentrate on the play and forget him. This just makes him worse. He dresses up in some ridiculous costume and comes and babbles and shrieks in our ear. Finally there is only one thing to do, and that is to shut down the play for awhile and try to talk to this guy. But it is not so easy, maybe he doesn't understand English too well or something, and two minutes of talking to him makes you feel like punching him in the mouth. The best thing to do is to see if someone knows this kook. No. 2 says he has seen him around, but not really to talk to, so that leaves No. 3. She must know him because she spends all that time backstage. The problem is what do we really know of her? She does her thing for a few minutes and goes off. Wait a minute. What *is* she doing with all that time backstage? You bet she knows him, probably all too well! Well, No. 3 is all we have. Maybe the play was getting a little old anyway. If we can get together with this maniac, I mean actor, then we could make a new play, something really different, a big hit. My name up in lights—darn—that little creep will probably demand top billing as well. Oh, well, the show must go on.

The 1st function, with the help of the 2nd and some of the 3rd, is at the center of ego-functioning in many normal adults. Normal adaptation is still a one-sided reality, for situations come up that demand a fuller adaptation than can be supplied by the conscious personality. The need for fuller adaptation is clearest at the critical points of our life when we are considering getting together with a partner, or when we reach certain turning points like career changes, middle age, etc. The ability to meet these needs comes from our ability to act with our total personalities and not just the conscious one. We need to integrate our personality to include the 3rd and 4th functions which are not presently conscious. The conscious must be brought into relationship with the unconscious, and a pivotal role in this process, which Jung called individuation, is played by the 4th function, for it is the most unconscious and most intimately bound up with the collective unconscious or the world within.

Individuation goes beyond the expansion of our consciousness. It is not simply the adding of more and more of the 2nd and 3rd and 4th functions to our 1st to create in effect a superpersonality according to the pattern of our 1st function, so that we would be more perceptive and effective and dynamic, etc. This is certainly one effect of working out our process of individuation, but our ego-consciousness is simply not the center of everything and cannot function as such. It lives between the world without and the world within, and these worlds are not subordinated to it. But if it acts as if they are, it becomes inflated with a false sense of its own particular importance and grandeur. Neither is the ego to be totally subordinated to these worlds. Such an assimilation leads to the loss of its own distinctive point of view and there is the danger of it being swallowed up.

In the 4th function we can see this process working itself out. The 4th function cannot be brought completely into the conscious personality. It is too loaded with the contents of the inner world, while at the same time the ego cannot just give up the distinctive point of view that it has through the 1st function. What happens is a process of accommodation where each yields and compromises. A new center is formed which is not to be identified with the old center of ego consciousness, but is a standpoint that tries to recognize the legitimate demands of both sides. The ego loses some of its one-sidedness and sees there are realities that go beyond it. It looks at the 4th function not as an annoyance but as a gateway to the world within with all its riches, as well as dangers. Then the 4th becomes a source of life. Jung called this new center the self.

The 4th is too distant from consciousness and too opposite in character to be approached directly. The 2nd and 3rd functions are the mediators. Often the 2nd or 3rd function is polarized by the attitude of the conscious in one part and the opposite attitude in the other part. There is a boundary, so to speak, which separates introversion from extraversion and conscious from unconscious. This boundary is not directly visible, for it touches the unconscious, which by definition means not visible to consciousness. It can be seen, however, in dreams in many different guises, and retrospectively. Once we have expanded our consciousness we can look back and see where the old boundary was.

The lower part of the 3rd function can form a bridge to the 4th, and the 4th in its turn allows us to deal with the relationship between the ego and the unconscious. The process of individuation happens in a distinctive way for each type, and naturally in a personal and individual way for each person.

Ways of Development of the Psychological Type

There are a number of basic ways in which to work on the development of our psychological type, and we will briefly summarize them here before we go on in chapter 5 to give some indications of the development of the 8 types according to body, temperament and psychological type.

1. Dreams. Dreams are graphic pictures of what the other side of our personality is like. They tend to compensate for our conscious one-sidedness and so if we pay attention to them they can give us a living picture of the struggle between conscious and unconscious, and the dominant and the least developed function. In them a drama is being played out which has to do with our instinctive urge to be whole and complete, and if we can understand the characters we can take a more decisive role in helping this process along. The more dreams in a series we possess, the more chance we have of finding clues in one dream that will help unravel another. One way which we can interpret dreams is from the perspective of our own type and how it is growing, and the problems it is facing.

Tom, an IUT Type.
Dream: Tom was in the back seat of a car and there was a strange man who was driving fast and somewhat recklessly. Tom's girlfriend was in the front passenger seat, and sometimes she would

turn around and hold Tom's hand, but at other times she flirted with the driver. Tom woke up with a feeling of anxiety about the possibility of losing his girlfriend. The strange man reminded him of the foreman on his last summer job whom Tom felt was coarse and loud.

Interpretation: The strange man symbolizes Tom's extraverted sensation function which is a stranger to consciousness and not particularly reliable. In contrast to Tom's conscious life which is directed by intuition, the dream shows the other side where the sensation function is in the driver's seat. The girlfriend can be understood as a symbol of Tom's 3rd function, feeling, which is pulled in 2 directions: on the one side towards the consciousness represented by Tom, and on the other towards the stranger. The feeling function is partially conscious and partially unconscious.

2. Daydreams. If we have recurrent daydreams and fantasies we can try to interpret them in the same fashion, for they are filled with material from the other side of our personality.

Daydream: Tom had a recurrent fantasy about being in a plane crash in a remote place. The crash had left the passengers with hardly any supplies and no ready means of help. It was Tom, drawing on his interior resources, who organized shelter using branches and leaves, found edible plants and took charge of the survival of the group. In the process of doing this, the most beautiful woman among the passengers was drawn to him because of his command of the situation.

Interpretation: The weakest part of Tom's personality is in the area of extraverted sensation. The daydream indicates that the function of intuition symbolized by the plane is no longer adequate. The unconscious, by means of the daydream, presents to him another Tom who is strong in this area and reaps the rewards of his strength. These images, coming from the unconscious, attempt to compensate for the one-sidedness of the conscious, and can be seen as an attempt to attract Tom to further self-development.

3. The Analysis of Moments of High Feeling Intensity. There are events in our lives that seem to strike us much more intensely than seems warranted by the actual facts of what happened. They are loaded with an extra charge of energy which comes not from the event itself but from the unconscious. The event has hit something there and released some of the energy the unconscious has, and the result is some kind of upset or depression or elation. If

we can discover what it is in the other side that is so energy-filled, we will get a new insight into what our other side is like. We can discover it by trying to write down the fantasies or associations it unleashes, or make a picture of it or in some fashion bring it to consciousness where we can then try to understand it.

A Moment of High Feeling Intensity: One day Tom was paging through a magazine and he read a short anecdote about a man who had spent 30 years in a mental hospital. The man had stated that the most fulfilling thing that had happened to him during all that time was that once, while working on the hospital newsletter, he had won an argument with the staff person in charge of the paper about how a particular word should be hyphenated. For some reason that Tom couldn't really fathom at the time, he couldn't forget that story.

Interpretation: The story symbolized in Tom's mind the possibility of being entrapped in the world, just like the mental patient had been locked up in the hospital. As an introverted intuition type, Tom loved freedom and feared that the details of sensation would tie him down and not let him fly. Tom was concerned about living a meaningful life, and was afraid that he would be caught in situations where fulfillment and meaning were hard to come by. The patient who had only one apparently trivial moment of fulfillment in 30 years symbolized Tom's fears.

4. Active Imagination. This is what Jung called the process of helping the unconscious communicate its contents to consciousness. We take a receptive attitude to this inner world and try to let it come through to us in the form most congenial to us. For some it is in the form of seeing images, for others it is in terms of hearing an inner voice, or shaping a piece of wood or clay or stone or even dancing. The idea is to let this other side have its say without immediately criticising it or repressing it if the contents seem banal or ugly or disagreeable. Once we have let it come out and elaborated it in terms of some concrete form, then we are in a position to try to understand it and to assert the rights of the ego to be heard, and in this way move towards a new center and a new way of functioning. There is a certain danger involved in all these methods, for they open the door to the unconscious contents, as we have mentioned before. If the unconscious contents were to come out too strongly, there is the possibility that people with a fundamental weakness in their psyche will find it very difficult to

control them. Profesional assistance is best for these cases. Sometimes the raw material for active imagination is right at hand, from daydreams and moments of high feeling intensity. At other times we have to take a receptive attitude and see what comes up.

> Active Imagination: Victor was in his early 50s and had just lost his wife about 6 weeks before. His grown children had been very supportive, but Victor felt he had to get away from the house and somehow try to cope with the intensely painful sense of loss that was in his thoughts almost constantly. He knew people expected him to snap out of it after a while, but so many things reminded him of his wife, and what he most wanted to do was have her back with him and talk to her. Victor knew he couldn't hide from the situation any longer. He needed to express his feelings. He started to talk to his wife and listen to what she might be saying in return. She was real inside of him, and so the conversation was far from being make-believe. He told her how much he missed her, and went on to share all the trials he had been going through. In turn, by way of active imagination, he allowed his wife in him to express how she felt. Bit by bit Victor began to come to terms with his loss.
>
> While it is true that Victor got support from his children and friends, he had to cope with the situation himself since it was his wife. He faced danger from 2 sides; the emotions in the unconscious were already activated, and could have a serious effect on his physical and psychic health if he did nothing about it and was continually weakened by the suffering it caused. On the other hand, he could not use the active imagination as a way to deny the reality of his wife's death without running the risk of serious psychological problems. He had to communicate with his wife to the degree that she was a living force within him, while realizing at the same time she was dead and he had to suffer the painful loss.

Jung and his collaborators have produced a rich body of literature about all these ways of relating to the unconscious. In the Notes for Further Study you can find some of the basic references. The more you use these means, the more you should study about them. Begin on a small scale so you can cope with the energy that is generated.

Visualizing Our Developed Type

We have within ourselves all the types on all 3 levels, and we can make use of this fact to get a preview of what full development means for our particular type. The way to do this is by imagining what we actually are like in one component of our type, and then imagining what it would be like to have less in that area and then more. This allows us to appreciate what we already have in comparison to what we could not have, and to get an idea of what full development means. This kind of imagination is not Jung's active imagination, for we are not trying to explicitly set up a dialogue with the unconscious. We are simply sketching out a blueprint for future development. We still have to build the house.

List your components on all 3 levels of type in order of strength, with the strongest first. Then take the 1st element and let yourself feel what it is actually like to have it. Then imagine if you were much weaker in this component. How would you get by? How would you do what you do now? How would the people around you like it? Be happy for the gift of what you have. Be sympathetic towards the people who are less well-endowed. Then imagine what it would be like to have even more of your 1st component. Would you like it? Would it be useful? Would it make life better? See if the extra endowment carries a price with it. Decide if you really would like more. If so, what are the strategies you could use to make the best possible use of what you have? Make use of the appropriate descriptions we have given to aid your imagination. Work your way through all the elements of your type in this manner. If in the course of these exercises in imagination some image or situation seems to have a lot of energy, i.e., it hits you, make a note of it, for it can be the beginning of a good process of active imagination.

Notes on Further Study

1. *Man and His Symbols* by Jung and his collaborators, is an excellent introduction to Jungian psychology, including the process of individuation.

2. *The Living Symbol, A Case Study in the Process of Individuation*, by Gerhard Adler, devotes 400 pages to one part of one person's inner development.

3. C. G. Jung's *The Relationship Between the Ego and the Unconscious* sums up the basic structure underlying the individual case material, while his *A Study of the Process of*

Individuation and *Concerning Mandala Symbolism* give an idea of how the new center of the personality emerges and what symbolic forms it takes.

4. Information about practicing Jungian analysts and Jungian organizations can be obtained from the C. G. Jung Training Center, 28 East 39th Street, New York, New York 10016; The Society of Analytical Psychology, 30 Devonshire Place, London, England WIN 1PE; and C. G. Jung Institut, Hornweg 28, 8700 Kusnacht, Switzerland.

Chapter 5

The Development of
the Eight Psychological Types

There is no prescription that will spell out how to develop your type. You are a certain type but in a particular and individual way. Your own path of development will be unique inasmuch as it draws on your personal history. No one will have your dreams or fantasies in exactly the same way. No one else will possess the foreign language of your inner world that you must learn to translate. So from this point of view there can be no set rules of behavior or dictionary of dream symbols that will relieve you of the task of exploring your inner world.

But if you go exploring without any compass or maps, you have a good chance of getting lost and in trouble. When Jung set out to travel in the unconscious, he had to fashion his compass as he went along. We, at least, can take advantage of his work and make our own journey safer. We have some tentative charts and landmarks to go by, but we still have to get up and go.

The following remarks on the development of the types, therefore, are not prescriptions to be handed out to each type, like advice dispensed from a fortune-telling machine. They are just hints about situations you might encounter in your own journey into the inner psyche.

The Development of the Extraverted Sensation Type

The Body Type

We have seen how the body type of the ES varies from the pole of predominant endomorphy to that of endomorphic mesomorphy. It is crucial to keep this in mind when reading the descriptions here which fit the more extreme endomorph and have to be more and more modified as the body type varies.

The ES type is the champion at eating and sleeping and relaxing. They love food, and have an almost irresistible tendency to gain weight, for they extract the maximum benefit from what they eat. Our present American diet of highly refined foods with the fiber removed and calories added is precisely the wrong diet for them. In an attempt to feel full they consume more calories than they use. A change of diet to a high fiber, low calorie diet with the right amount of protein and vitamins is a step in the right direction, for it will give a sense of fullness without the drawbacks of too many calories. Another step is in the form of having two meals a day instead of three.

The weight problem of the ES is aggravated by his low metabolism and his inclination to relaxation. He does not burn up energy in muscular tension or in exercise as readily as other types. This means more weight, which in turn leads to less exercise and still more weight. For the ES who is high in endomorphy but low in mesomorphy, getting enough exercise is a difficult task. Exercise in this context does not have to mean jogging or calisthenics, but simply direct physical action like walking to the corner store and working in the garden, etc. Swimming is not only a well-rounded form of exercise, but endomorphs do well at it because of their buoyancy.

The ES who is high in mesomorphy often combines a high level of direct physical action and exercise and excessive weight. The weight is more spread out and less noticeable in appearance, but the combination still tends to overload him. This somatotype territory is prone to coronary heart disease. See chapter 9 for further details about Type and Coronary Heart Disease.

The ES likes to sleep and does well at it. He is therefore inclined to oversleep, which, of course, does little to help the weight problem. The primary endomorphy of the ES tends to buffer them from the full development of their ectomorphic component. We have described this component as a need for quiet and sense of listening. The endomorph is biologically introverted with his energies focused on his physical well-being. This is in sharp contrast with the biological extraversion of the ectomorph whose body is exposed to all sorts of stimuli like a giant disk antenna. The endomorph is compact and has proportionally less of this receptive ability. Therefore, he needs to make a special effort to have a definite quiet time to help in his listening to these more distant messages, which often carry important information about his inner self.

The Temperament Type

The ES type displays a wonderful extraversion of affect by which he makes other people feel at ease because of his own amiability, complacency and tolerance. He tends to be open-hearted and open-handed, and have a strong sense of family. But these positive qualities do not exist in a vacuum. They are linked with the less developed aspects of the same temperament.

Unless ESs are high in mesomorphy, they tend to lack a certain drive and discipline to get jobs done. Their habit of amiable acceptance makes it hard for them to be consistent disciplinarians. Their open-handedness with their money leads to budgetary problems. They can profit from making a budget or a list of chores for their children or themselves, to make what is to be done more tangible and objective, and hopefully more achievable, but the roots of the problem lie deeper than this.

The very sociability of the ES is linked with his difficulty in making use of quiet time to reflect about himself. His biological introversion is compensated by a psychological extraversion. He likes, needs and wants to have people around. But this extraversion makes it more difficult for him to deal with his introverted side, which has to do with reflection about the goals of his own personal life. The ES who takes an hour to go for a walk by himself, or to sit in a quiet place, not to meet everyone or notice everything, but simply to be alone and have a gentle inward focus, may find that this practice allows him to deal with his own personal decision-making better and consider where he has come from and where he is going. This kind of active listening is not to be confused with a passive feeling of inertia that might be related to the sense of depression sometimes found in this type.

The ES type on the body and temperament level possesses virtues, but these virtues are connected with vices, or to put it into another language, each positive quality is linked with an undeveloped or even negative quality, and real development is a process of forming a new center which takes both sides into account. ESs can eat well and do so, but this good quality often leads to overeating which has an effect on their physical and social well-being. Instead of eating being brought to the temperamental level in the form of a social sacrament of eating, where they are at the table with their friends and family in good fellowship, they incur social disapproval and are called fat people. This leads to guilt and secret eating. The wonderful sense of relaxation and tolerance of other people that they possess as a natural attribute can lead to their being the victims of intolerance where they are called shiftless and lazy. Their heart-warming flow of feeling towards other people can have its negative side as well, where they find themselves being fended off for being excessively sentimental and affectionate.

All the other types have problems, each in his own way, and each type cannot reach a full measure of growth and happiness simply by depending upon their most conscious and developed gifts, without the development of the weaker and less conscious part of his personality.

The Psychological Type

The possibilities of development are even more ample at the level of psychological type, and here the balancing of the various components takes a deeper meaning and leads to a new center of personality.

The extraversion of affect we saw at the level of temperament becomes transformed into extraverted sensation. Extraversion of affect is not to be confused with Jung's extraverted feeling. The feeling of the ES follows in the path of the sensation function. His feeling is at the service of the ES energy, and so it does not have the focused quality of the EF. Sheldon could say that they like people simply because they are people. The ES's enjoyment of people does not depend upon careful discrimination about the people whom they are enjoying.

The use of the auxiliary functions allows the ES to discriminate and evaluate and follow through on their objects of interest. In this way, the 2nd and 3rd functions of either thinking or feeling are equivalent on this level to what mesotonia is on the level of temperament. It is the feeling and the thinking functions, to the degree they are aiding the 1st function, that let him acquire the drive and discipline and active pursuit of the outer goal that will allow him not only to sense what is around him but to act on this perception for his own good. The higher the mesotonic component in the ES type, the easier this energetic action is to begin with. An EST or ESF finds some difficulty in learning to use the 3rd function, for it is another way of evaluating things, and they are used to the old way. The ESF, for example, who has good social follow-through, has to work at developing a logical follow-through that is useful in other situations.

Somewhere in the functions is the door that leads to the introverted side of the personality. Depending on age and stage of development it could be anywhere from the upper part of the 1st function to the lower part of the 4th. Often it is somewhere in the 3rd in many adults. They have conscious use of the 1st, some of the 2nd, and a bit of the 3rd. When this is not true, the process of development takes a different course, for the 2nd and 3rd functions need to be more integrated before the problem of the other side can be tackled.

Since the 4th function of the personality is the least known, we cannot turn directly to it and try to draw it into consciousness. The lower part of the 3rd, which would be either introverted feeling or introverted thinking, forms the bridge to the introverted intuition. It is here that we need the various methods that we have discussed, namely dreams, fantasies, experiences of high feeling intensity and active imagination. Any one of these 4 methods can provide access to what is happening in the world below. Once we gain some insight we must not simply look at it but try to figure out what practical steps we can take to integrate it into our lives.

The Extraverted Thinking Type

The Body Type

On the whole ETs are energetic and active. No one has to be after them to get exercise. Their high energy output lessens the chance of them becoming overweight. However, when they dwell in the territory right next to the ES boundary they can put on pounds and their drive which can be even more intense than the ES can lead to health difficulties. See *Type and Coronary Heart Disease* in chapter 9.

The more mesomorphic the ET is, the less he shares the endomorph's love of food and his relaxed style of eating and digesting. The ET often eats infrequently and voraciously, and is not inclined to sit and relax or spend much time sleeping. He gets by on the least sleep of all the types. The ET has to learn how to let his endomorphic component come out. He should take time for regular, well-prepared meals, preferably with other people, and spend some time eating and socializing without trying to do something else as well. He can benefit from just sitting and letting himself relax. This relaxation can be a way of approaching the question of time for himself and listening to his inner demands. The relentless drive of the ET to accomplish his plans conflicts with the conditions he needs in order to see what his plans are doing to him on a personal level. An all-consuming plan can bring him to a state of ruining his health and alienating the people around him. On the basic level of ectomorphy he has to stop and take time to listen to his own inner demands and those of the people he loves.

The Temperament Type

The ET excels in direct decisive action in the face of obstacles without which many jobs in this world would be left undone. But this positive aspect is connected with a negative one. Decisive action becomes ruthlessness; direct execution becomes callousness to the feelings of others, and a love of challenge becomes a love of domination.

Mesotonia must leave room for endotonia. The ET needs to spend time with his family and friends without constantly looking at his watch or sitting on the edge of his seat. He can profit by trying to like people because they are people without considering how they fit into his plans. The endotonic Sunday dinner with the whole family around the table is not a bad place to start.

Mesotonia must also come to terms with ectotonia. It is only with a modicum of privacy and freedom from incessant pressures that the ET can listen to the messages coming from his own body and psyche. He needs time to dream and focus on the world within. This inner world holds the answer to psychic growth and health.

The Psychological Type

We have already described the basic structure of the ET with his 1st function and how the 2nd and 3rd serve to strengthen it. The first phase of development is this strengthening and expanding of ego consciousness. This often happens more or less naturally as we grow up and try to use our best talents to make our way in the world around us. Unfortunately the very kind of specialization and differentiation of functions that allow us to play a part in society leads us to one-sidedness in our personal development. The ET must develop the auxiliary functions, but this alone will not lead to complete development.

The second phase of development deals with the question of the 4th function and the relationship between the ego and the unconscious. This kind of development is not fostered in the same way by the world we live in. It is not as immediately evident that we are undeveloped in this sense, for we can carry out a normal role in society without it, but it does make a great deal of difference in terms of our personal health and happiness and the state of psychic health of the world in general.

The ET often uses the lower part of the 3rd function to make contact with the 4th. He has to be careful that he does not try to simply rope it into consciousness. For example, the intuition of the ETS is partially allied to the conscious personality, and as such is a source of valuable new ideas. When he approaches and contacts a deeper part of the intuitive function he is liable to expect it to produce more new ideas that will be of use in his overall conscious plan. The real value of the introverted part of the intuitive 3rd function lies in what it can say about the ultimate meaning of life rather than the help it can give in starting a new business. It is only by overcoming great inward resistances that the ETS can accept as a reality this kind of message. Introverted intuition which contemplates the goals and purposes of the inner life must be accepted as such and the ETS must ask himself, "What purpose does my inner life have?" "What is to become of all that I have?" "What is the purpose of being?" When these sorts of questions become real questions, they lead to introverted feeling by which he faces the question, "What is it that these kinds of values have to say to me?" "What does the love I have for my wife and family really mean to me?" In this way the inner world begins to open up, and if it is accepted and taken seriously, it modifies the conscious personality and its behavior. The new and the old personality find a new common center of gravity to revolve around.

The Introverted Intuition Type
The Body Type

There is a considerable range in the body type of the IU, as we have seen, and each of these somatotypes would have a different developmental path, but with some common characteristics. The ectomorph has a finely-tuned nervous system, and a highly developed self-awareness. With this radar he is constantly picking up not ordinary sense impressions but signals from beyond his immediate environment. He is a biologically extraverted organism, and his acute perception of these signals comes at the price of tending to be abstracted from concrete sense details.

The more unbuffered by endomorphy he is, the more he must protect himself from overstimulation. His nervous system can become overloaded in situations that other types take for granted, e.g. by crowds, shopping trips, noise. They have the highest need for quiet of all the types.

The ectomorph without endomorphy tends to have a short length of intestines, a small stomach, a high basal metabolism rate and a considerable energy output from muscular tension and a highly charged nervous system. Therefore he needs a high protein, high calorie, easily digestible diet with frequent feedings of smaller portions. Breakfast is important so as not to draw down his energy supply. The IU who is an endomorphic ectomorph, on the other hand, will tend to be overweight like the ES, and would need to follow a more ES-type diet.

The ectomorph is often a light sleeper and a poor one; he can use a full 8 hours, and sometimes a catnap during the day is helpful in order to give his awareness a rest. The same purpose can be served by some light distracting recreation. Even with a lot of sleep ectomorphs can suffer from a chronic sense of fatigue and be depressed from no other cause but low energy. He must protect his energy supply both from overstimulaton and overexercise. In contrast to the mesomorph, instead of a real workout invigorating him, it can leave him moping around for the rest of the day. Some exercise, in a non-jarring form, like cycling or Yoga or walking, can be very beneficial in bringing out the mesomorphic side. The ectomorph, when he is extreme, needs to carry what weight he can as a form of padding, and make judicious use of social contact and exercise as a way to bring him out of himself without causing

74

exhaustion. In cases of exhaustion caused by overstimulation, the IU often responds to solitude and quiet.

The Temperament Type

The IU is the most ectotonic of the psychological types. They put first the development and the continuity of their inner awareness. They are constantly receiving inputs from within and without, from both far and near via their intuition. If they are to receive their faint, distant signals, they must shield themselves from excessively strong stimulation in the foreground. They spend their energy linking up their new feelings and thoughts, intuitions and sensations to the past with the desire to be able to grasp past, present and future in one unitary gaze. They tend to be aware of their fantasy and dream life which form integral parts of their extended consciousness and are a source of new intuitions. This process of inner exploration has both a positive and a negative side. On the positive side they often pick up interesting and valuable information about the meaning and purpose of the inner man. But on the negative side, they can carry the process of inhibition of the endotonic and the mesotonic components to excess. The IU has a tendency to withdraw too much from people. He becomes too wrapped up in his inner world and has no time for normal social contacts. He becomes reclusive and aloof, and people sensing these qualities feel rebuffed and rebuff him in return, but he sees only their rejection and not the reason for it. He uses it for justification to socially isolate himself even more. This does not mean that the IU would enjoy the same social gatherings as the ES, but in his own way he needs people around him. These contacts usually take the form of a few good friends where deep relationships develop.

The IU has a tendency not to act, or put it another way, he is very active mentally but slow to act physically, especially when faced with a repetitive physical task. He tends to hold himself aloof from ordinary chores, partly because he is oblivious to them and partly because he feels he is engaged interiorly in something more important. It is as if he has to disengage his attention and specially focus it on the external job to be done before he can react and do it. He cannot withdraw from the physical world and live exclusively within. He should make a special effort to become competent in those skills which most of the rest of the world take for granted, like cooking, building a bookcase, doing minor repairs on his car, etc. These are all ways of developing the mesotonic extraversion of action. Naturally the more mesomorphic IUs will tend to have less problems with doing things, but more problems with people, while with the more endomorphic IUs, the tendency will be reversed. The balanced IUs with a good endowment of each of the three temperamental components are often very capable in all areas, but suffer from an inability to choose what they really want to do.

The Psychological Type

The IU who does not make use of his 2nd function of either thinking or feeling can wander in a world of interior images or ideas without trying to organize or evaluate them. A more systematic approach to the inner possibilities helps counterbalance the urge to be always running to see what is beyond the next interior hill. The IU needs to make the attempt to discover the basic structure and interrelationships in the mass of inner images and ideas that usually present themselves to him. This makes the inner world more useful to him when he acts upon it and communicates it.

Whether he likes it or not, and he often doesn't, the IU lives in this world and must learn how to relate to it. The IU has already developed a way of relating to the world as he grew up by use of his conscious functions, which Jung called a persona, but his persona could never answer the question of "What is really my place in this world?" or "Can I really have a life in this world without it contradicting my inner world?" The answer to these questions is related to the integration of the other side of the personality. The bridge to the other side is often either extraverted feeling or extraverted thinking with overtones of sensation. The overtones spring from the connection the 3rd function has with the extraverted sensation of the 4th. The other side when unintegrated manifests itself in a fear of being engulfed and enslaved by the world.

The extraverted nature of the 3rd function often presents itself in the form of having an actual relationship with someone of the opposite sex, and the challenge of the 4th function can be found in dealing directly with simple sensation realities. For the more extraverted type, these ordinary everyday things seem hardly worth noting, but for the IU, because the 4th function is filled with the unconscious, they can have a mysterious and frightening quality which makes it very difficult to deal with them in a straight-forward objective manner.

The Extraverted Intuition Type
The Body Type

The EUs are highly active people, for they not only have something new they must be doing but they have the mesomorphy to sustain their extraverted action. Often they will not take time to eat properly and they have their meals on the run. The lack of a proper diet probably accentuates their changeability; they lack the endomorph's weight which might have slowed them down a bit. They also lack the endomorph's bodily relaxation. Their muscles are in a state of tension as if they must be ready to charge off at a moment's notice. A set time for meals together, with a carefully chosen balanced diet, with the meals eaten without a sense of rush, are all good goals for the more extreme EU.

EUs share the IU's fascination for new possibilities, but not his inclination for quiet time. Quiet time for themselves is about last on their list of priorities, but this is the doorway to the world within. They have to learn to stop so the body and psyche can catch up.

The Temperament Type

The EUs can be pleasant company, for they can be bubbling over with new adventures and they have a knack of projecting their feelings into a social situation and warming it much like the EF. This is not the more diffused amiability of the ES; it is more highly focused and in the service of the primary intuition. They tend to turn their feelings on and off according to whether the situation has intuitive possibilities for them or not. They have to learn that their friends want a constancy of feeling tone and attention even when they themselves are in a rush to be off on new adventures.

Their ectotonia is bound up with their intuition rather than their self-reflection. This they tend to avoid like their brother extraverts, and their highly-tuned antenna is outwardly directed rather than inwardly, as with the IU. Their constant future orientation does not give them time to reflect on what is happening to their lives here and now under the impact of the headlong rush. They need time for their ectotonia to assert itself so they can see what price the people around them are paying, as well as the burden their own body is carrying.

The Psychological Type

The EU, even with the aid of the helping functions, cannot really deal with his other side effectively, for all these functions have an extraverted character to the degree they are integrated with the conscious personality. This same sort of cleavage exists in all the types, and the initial reorientation of attitude is one of the most decisive battles that must be fought. The conscious attitude has become solidified over the years so that the habitual way of dealing with problems is in terms of more of the same. What is necessary is a new attitude, but this feels like an affront and insult to consciousness, and so it is resisted. For the EU the other side is characterized by introverted thinking or feeling and introverted sensation. Instead of letting introverted sensation batter him from the outside, the EUT has to try to approach it through the mediation of the lower 3rd function which asks, "How do I personally feel about all these intuitions?" "How can I evaluate them for myself?" And deeper down he has to submit to letting himself look at his sense impressions in order to establish a relationship to his inner world through them.

The Introverted Sensation Type
The Body type

The IS with his ectomorph-endomorph physique is inclined to put on extra weight, but not apparently to the extent of the ES. The extra weight, however, is enough to increase the inhibition of his mesomorphic component which is already being held in check by the introverted sensation itself. The IS is often a slow reactor, and he does not need any extra obstacles.

The IS shares the ectomorph's love of quiet, but most of the quiet is taken up with sense impressions which do not incline them to movement in the way the intuitions of the IU often spill over into going somewhere new. The IS has to be careful not to build a cocoon from which he has difficulty emerging.

The Temperament Type

The ISs show little of the open love of people of the ES. They have good feeling tone, but often find it difficult to express these feelings freely and be demonstrative with them. They have to work at being more dramatic than their personal inclination, based on a realization that the world around them measures feeling by the extraverted feeling of the EF and the ES, and so has difficulty believing that they really do have feelings at all.

They work in a highly meticulous and organized way. Their own experience of working with other people should be enough to show them that their work style differs from others. This should be accepted as a simple fact without judging if the other person is doing a good job by the exacting IS standards. There are other standards that have to do with speed, sociability while working, etc., which if they cannot emulate because of their own gift, they can learn to appreciate and thus lessen the tension of working with other types.

The Psychological Type

The IS with the help of the 2nd and 3rd functions makes his way in the world as a good and steady worker. This is the persona that he presents, his extraverted mask, while beneath it he lives in his introverted world. But neither the persona nor the conscious introverted personality is fully adequate for all the situations. The IS can be stuck in his current situation because of inertia and a lack of development of the other side which would give him access to more extraverted energies, particularly extraverted intuition.

Often the development of the other side of the introverts, since it has an extraverted character, is associated with outer events.

For the IS and IU courtship and marriage can represent a difficult challenge precisely because it is not a matter-of-fact reality, but intimately linked with their 3rd function of extraverted feeling or thinking which is often quite undeveloped. The development of the other side of the introvert is not simply the adjustment to the demands of the outer world but a simultaneous development of a deeper part of his personality which he needs in order to make the outer adjustment.

Extraverted feeling or thinking is the bridge to dealing with extraverted intuition for the IS. And the EU is the way the IS not only deals with questions of "What new job should I take?" or "What new life-style should I adopt?", but it is also at the same time the medium by which the IS deals with the legitimate demands of the inner world and begins to balance the one-sidedness of consciousness with a relationship to both the outer and inner world.

The Extraverted Feeling Type

The Body Type

The EF has many similarities with the ET as we have already noted. She does not have to be told to exercise, but weight gain for those along the ES line is equally dangerous to her health. They share the ET's lack of quiet time, and as more and more EFs enter the male competitive arenas they will tend to show the ET's difficulty in relaxing, sleeping, taking time to eat, etc. Hopefully their higher degree of endomorphy will help keep them from the worst excesses.

The Temperament Type

The EF with too little to do, either because she is held back by stereotypes about women's roles in the world or by her own inability to think up what to do, has no real outlet for her mesotonia. Her ability for energetic action can be frittered away on inconsequential activities and leave her unsatisfied. The EF who takes her place in the world alongside the ET avoids this problem, but has to face the problems of the working mesotonic.

The mesotonic in a career position can develop tunnel vision and compulsive drive that begins to ignore the enjoyment of people because they are people and family as family, and subordinate everything to the job to be done. There is even less opportunity for time for reflection on inner goals and not just time to rest and recharge batteries for more work.

The emphasis on mesotonia in the EF gives rise to the paradox of the unfeeling feeler, which is the counterpart of the ruthlessness and callousness sometimes found in the ET. The extraverted feeling becomes more and more one-sided and since it is cut off from the rest of the personality, it lacks new creative energies and becomes narrower and narrower in application. It loses a certain flexibility of being nice in general and becomes nice for definite motives, and thus appears calculating and cold when seen from outside the focus of feeling attention.

The Psychological Type

The other side of the EF is introverted thinking, which is approached by either introverted sensation or introverted intuition. Both of these approaches take time and reflection in order to perceive what the contents of the inner world are, and that these contents are as worthy of attention as the outer world. The EF is quick to find substitutes for her own thought. She tends to take up as her own what society thinks. If this process is not broken by inner development, then a change of social setting does not necessarily lead to meaningful change, but simply to the adoption of another ready-made body of thought. The EF has to reach the point of saying, "What do I really think?" "What is my personal philosophy of life?" This is very different from taking up some philosophy ready-made and saying, "This is my philosophy now." A personal standpoint has to be worked out step-by-step by a dialogue between the conscious and the unconscious. The result might be of modest size, but it will be real and effective for the person who has created it.

The Introverted Thinking and the Introverted Feeling Types

The Body Type

We have seen the wide divergence of body types that distinguishes the ITU from the ITS and the IFU from the IFS. The ITU shares many of the problems of the IUT, especially if his ectomorphy is pronounced. He has more mesomorphy and thus can sustain exercise better, but he should tend to a modified version of the IUT sleep and diet habits. This holds as well for the IFU of high ectomorphy. Extra weight and relaxation will help them express their low endomorphic component better, and protect them from overstimulation.

The ITS and the IFS have a tendency to put on weight and become heavy-set or beefy, and can follow a modified version of the ES diet. Both the ITS, IFS and the ITU, IFU value quiet and privacy.

The Temperament Type

The ITs show little of the indiscriminate amiability of the endotonic. This is more noticeable in the ITS than it is in the ITU, for we instinctively expect the more endomorphic personality to express more amiability. ITSs have a strong mesotonic component, but it is expressed not in the action of the ET but in a mental way. They are decisive thinkers and careful planners and make formidable competitors. They have to strive to allow their endotonia to come out, and simply enjoy the people around them, especially in the forms that are most distant to inner intellectuality like children, pets, etc.

The IFS and the IFU are blessed with abundant feelings, but since they flow inwardly, they have to make an extra effort to let their endotonia come out and let the people around them know that they have feelings by vocalizing and demonstrating them.

The Psychological Type

The ITs with thinking aided by the 2nd and 3rd functions can be effective and efficient both within his world of ideas and in their application. His persona of the thinking man is appreciated in our society. The IFs, however, seem to have more difficulty because they are judged more critically according to the EF norms of society. Their persona often appears less adequately developed from this point of view.

But the ITs and the IFs, in common with the rest of the introverts, need to make a more adequate contact with the outer world than what their one-sided persona allows. This contact and adaptation to the outer world is simultaneously one of relation to the inner world as well. There are situations which will demand an extraverted 3rd function of sensation or intuition, as well as contact with an extraverted 4th function of feeling or thinking as the case may be.

The ITs must develop the ability to consciously contact their EF side and use it to maintain the feeling tone with the people around them, especially those outside of their inner circle. The IFs must develop the ET dimension of their personality, which, on the outside, represents the ability to plan and act effectively and logically and see how the world works, and thus avoid succumbing to a magical kind of thought which grips them and takes the place of real thinking. But the 4th function in each is not simply a way of better outer adaptation; it is the path of inner adaptation as well, and through it the ITs answer the questions "How do I feel about myself?" "What are my values for my own life?" And the IFs develop their personal philosophies, much like we have seen in the case of the EF.

Work and Play and the 4th Function

The 4th or inferior function presents problems uniquely its own. It is the furthest removed from consciousness, and it is the bridge or doorway to the unconscious. It is united to the unconscious in such a way that it cannot be wholly disengaged and brought to consciousness. It will always have a more capricious and less reliable aspect than the other functions. This is why the approach to the 4th function cannot be a simple business approach by which we desire to use it for the practical work in which the conscious personality is engaged in. The 4th function has to be approached with a certain spirit of play and leisure so that it can express itself and emerge on its own terms without immediately being repressed or pressed into service for ego-oriented goals. One person might take up painting, another sculpture or playing in the sand or dancing, etc., all of which could serve as ways to express the 4th function and through it the unconscious.

But the 4th function is an integral part of our total way of adapting to reality. In order to be truly functional in this world we need both attitudes and all 4 functions. Therefore, we cannot think that simply by molding clay for an hour or two a week that we have developed our 4th function to a sufficient degree. Full development calls for using all the functions. If we try to make the more conscious functions bridge the gap left by the absence of the 4th, it would be like a table with three legs that never has the stabilty that it was meant to have. The 4th leg can be put into place even though it might be a little shorter than the others. We need the 4th function operative day-by-day on a practical level, even though it will remain weaker than the other functions and be always commingled to a certain degree with the unconscious. Our vision will never be perfectly in focus with the 4th function, but we have to use it nonetheless and be resigned to the tricks it will play on us, and the reminders it will give us that it still remains inferior in development to the other functions.

We cannot expect the IU to do without ES and simply have the thinking and feeling function take up the gap. The IU lives on this earth and needs to be in contact with it. In the same way we cannot expect the ES to do without IU, for they have inner personal goals to fulfill. From this point of view the 4th function is more than an area where you play and set up an artificial situation in which it can emerge, though the importance of this is not to be denied. After play comes work, but here we have to walk the narrow line between asking the 4th to do too much or too little. In a world of specialization where large numbers of people are concentrating on the strength of their superior function, it is too much to expect someone to use their inferior function to create a business or earn a living with it. This can put too much strain on it. For example, it would be a great deal to ask of a highly ectomorphic IU that he become a carpenter and professional builder of houses. But it might not be too much to ask him to build his own house, even though he needs freedom and leisure, in short the right surroundings and sense of security in which to build it. This is a long way from leaving him with the impression that the only castles he will build are on the beach or in the air. In a similar manner it would be a mistake to expect the IT to be the master of ceremonies at social functions, or the smooth host at a party. However, the IT has a family and a community to relate to on the feeling level, and though this is an obligation he has to fulfill in his own unique fashion, he must fulfill it nonetheless.

The problem of the 4th will not just disappear, but it can be greatly mitigated in its negative aspects and utilized in its positive ones as a source of new life. When a new center representing the whole personality forms, we can act out of that center in a way which, while it does not do away with our type, does allow us to respond to different situations with different functions and attitudes without us being completely identified with any one function. We can pick up the functions and attitudes we need because we rest in a center that is not completely identified with any one of them. When we are done with them we put them down, without fear that we will lose them. This will not make them of equal strength, but we will have reached a certain kind of wholeness and maturity.

The 4th function with its particular kind of difficulties can sometimes appear at the time Jung called the second half of life. Around our 35-37th year, though it can be earlier or later, we reach our second half of life. Up until this point our energy has been directed outwardly to things like education, career, marriage and family, home and material security. Let us suppose we have been modestly successful in accomplishing these goals which represent the externals of being an adult in our society. Then one day, much to our surprise, we find that we don't have the energy we used to have for these same things. We are puzzled by our lack of enthusiasm and wonder if we are somehow losing our grip. A fear of slipping can lead us to intensify the use of our one-sided consciousness, and this in turn makes us feel even emptier. Our sense of dissatisfaction can be projected outward in the search for a new mate or a new career, but it will remain unresolved as long as the question of the total development of the personality is neglected, and at the heart of this development is the 4th function.

It appears that extraverts and introverts undergo the second half of life in different ways. The extraverts have often concentrated on outer adaptation and need to turn within, but introverts, while they also need to integrate the other side of their personality, are already inward-looking, and this deeper integration can go hand-in-hand with a better adaptation to outer events.

Sheldon noted that ectotonics are often late maturers, as opposed to mesotonics who mature early. Ectotonics often marry late, make career choices later on in life and mature mentally and flower well into middle age. They give the appearance of being less adapted to outer events, but this lack of adaptation can be seen in a positive light as well. The ectotonic, in order to deal with an outer event, must deal with the inner impact and implications of that event as well, and if he can adapt to the outer event, it will tend to be a more complete adaptation. It can take him longer to get to something, but his arrival might well be more secure and far-reaching. From the perspective of the development of psychological types it is possible that both introverts and extraverts have equal advantages, each in their own way, in coping with the second half of life. The introvert could well have been dealing with the questions of the other side of the personality much of his adult life, but slowly and in connection with his problems of outer adaptation, while the extravert arrives at the second half of life with a firmer grasp of outer adaptation, yet has fewer clues about what inner adaptation means. However, if he can get through the initial transition, he might well concentrate on it with the same kind of whole-hearted dedication he previously gave to his relationship with the outer world.

It would be a mistake to imagine that the distinctions made in this chapter in terms of paths of development represent an exact picture of what happens in the unconscious itself. The unconscious is a living reality, and is alive with many different impulses and vital inner instincts towards wholeness. These go on continually as witnessed by our dreams that speak night after night whether we listen or not. This process cannot reach its goal if there are obstacles in the way, but it will keep on trying. It would not be surprising to discover that we are always dreaming, as Jung suggested, but during the day our consciousness is so bright that it blots out the dreams much like the sun blots out the stars. What is important is not the theory of development we follow but that we actually grow.

How to Develop Your Own Type

1. Try to get a detailed practical picture of how far your actual conscious development extends. How much do you make use of your 2nd function? How much of the 3rd? And the 4th? This means as part of your equipment day-by-day in facing life.

2. Determine what function is split the most by the line separating the conscious and unconscious. What is the function that is polarized into opposite attitudes? This is the place to start to build a bridge over to the other side. Look for actual examples of this split in your dreams and in things that have happened to you.

3. See how this split function is connected with the one underneath it.

4. With this concrete awareness of the actual state of your psychic health, it is much easier to try to improve it. Look for strategies that will lessen the conflict. Try to work on it both inside and out: inside by a process of active imagination, the study of dreams, etc., and outside by pursuing concrete tasks.

Chapter 6

Types Together

The best preparation for dealing with people of other types is to have dealt with the types within yourself. If you can see in a personal and practical manner how you are a community of types with strengths and weaknesses, you can see other people more clearly, for they, too, are not simple types but totalities. It is all too easy to succumb to putting a superficial label on our fellow man instead of going through the hard work of trying to understand him. Even if this label reads EU or IS, it will not solve our conflicts with others unless we are striving to heal these conflicts within ourselves. This superficial form of characterization always upset Jung, for he felt that it often missed the reality of types as an inner dynamic process of individuation. Types can be used to explore relationships, and Jung himself used them in this way in trying to help explain husbands to wives, parents to children, etc., but we have to be continually on our guard against losing sight of the complex realities they represent, and settling simply for the naming of the most conscious function.

Types and Tolerance

If you understand the nature of typology, this fact alone is a big step towards making you more tolerant, even though you are not certain what the other person's type is. The beginning of tolerance comes from the recognition of the existence of legitimate diversities among people. You realize there is the possibility of understanding someone's conduct and you can view it as a task to be accomplished rather than an intolerable annoyance. You can realize that you have something in common with the other person, even if it means reaching into the less developed parts of your personality in order to find it, and you can be alert to appreciate his talents because they can help you become stronger.

Types and Stereotypes

We often see the people around us through the colored glasses of our conscious function. Yet we believe that we are being totally objective. Objectivity is a goal we strive towards, but not only is our conscious way of looking at things tinted by our own dominant attitude and function but the other less developed types within ourselves are having their say and effecting how we see people without us realizing it.

As we have seen, though parts of ourselves are unconscious, that does not prevent them from getting us into trouble, and part of their mischief is to make the people around us appear different from the way they actually are. Why does the unconscious do that? Simply because it is trying to find a way to bring itself to our attention, and if we won't look within, it will go outside and approach us from there. This process is called projection. Projection occurs on the level of body and temperament, as well as psychological type. It is useful to look at it in oversimplified and exaggerated form. In actual practice it hovers around the edge of consciousness and forms a subtle atmosphere of pre-judgment without becoming fully conscious.

The mesomorph looks at the endomorph as fat and self-indulgent. *"Why don't they get up and work?" "Why don't they sweat some of that weight off instead of hanging around belly-aching?"* He sees them through a haze of half-formed opinions as soft and self-indulgent mesomorphs who have to learn the value of discipline.

The mesomorph sees the ectomorph as basically useless; someone who is sitting on the sidelines of life, who is no threat but doesn't do anything either. *"Who knows what goes on in their mind? A bunch of dreamers at best and at worst loners who you would not be surprised turned out to be involved in some kind of shady business. They are intellectuals who have driven themselves crazy by thinking too much and might lash out in some act of violence."* They are stunted and twisted mesomorphs.

The ectomorphs view the endomorphs with a measure of distaste; indulgent mountains of flesh without refinement, wallowing in sense pleasures and gushing and slobbering over each other; a bunch of crude individuals lounging in front of the blaring T.V.s; big mouths.

They see the mesomorphs as rude and selfish. Pushy and aggressive people who think they belong at the front of the line. Talking loud and making crude remarks and riding rough shod over everything in their way to get what they want. A bunch of spoilers destroying the earth to get their loot, and starting fights on any pretext.

The endomorphs view the mesomorphs as unfeeling and uncaring savages who lack normal friendliness and compassion. Always on the go without time for manners or decent amenities. People with no real friends.

They see the ectomorphs as cold fish who never have had any feelings and aren't about to get any; proud people going around as if they were better than anyone else, who think they are too good for normal talk, uppity intellectual snobs who are off in some corner up to no good.

The Psychological Types

For the extravert the introvert is painfully shy and socially backward, stuck in himself and unwilling or unable to come out into the healthy sunshine and enjoy life. He is melancholic and brooding, preoccupied with self to such a degree that it can lead only to morbidity and dark deeds.

For the introvert the extravert is all bluster and show, a whirlwind of action and talk who tries to hide the fact that there is no substance to him. He is a hollow man, who has given up his soul to run after trifles. He is frivolous or flighty, or worse, overbearing and tyrannical.

The sensation type can feel that the intuition type does not have his feet on the ground. He is flying off into a fantasy world at the least provocation while he ignores the most basic facts of life like proper meals, cleanliness, earning a living, and the other realities of living in this world.

The intuition type often sees the sensation type in the guise of a carnal man stuck in his immediate environment and preoccupied with eating and sleeping and dressing and working, all to excess, and whose idea of fun is some dreary repetitive game, without knowing any of the excitement of higher things.

The feeler type looks on the thinker as a cold inhuman computer who would rather be with numbers or machines or fancy ideas than with people. The thinker appears rigid and uncaring and without heart, and a living time bomb when you do manage to drag him into a social gathering.

For the thinking type the feeler is above all else unreasonable. She is constantly off on emotional tangents or pestering you to death with her entreaties or complaints or just plain gushing in a way which is impervious to good sense and a clear statement of position.

Naturally these sketches are exaggerated, and we could make more refined ones and focus on other kinds of opposition, like that between the ES and the IU, or the ET and the IF. However, this gives the general idea, and the more precise examples should be your own. Think of the people you have an instinctive dislike for, a dislike at first sight. What type are they? Turn to Figure 3 and see what type is the most opposite to your own. How do you feel about that particular type of person?

The simple recognition of our particular inclinations to prejudice is an important first step in eradicating them. The real process of becoming unprejudiced is in our healing of the splits that exist in our own personality so that they will not be projected outward. We will return to the question of projection after we look at how our own type has been shaped by the people and society around us.

Types and Environment

From the moment we are conceived we are being molded and shaped by the environment around us. We can imagine the type we are born with to be a particular kind of seed. If we are a lettuce we should not expect to be transformed into a tomato or a cabbage or even another variety of lettuce. But this does not make our environment unimportant. The environment is like the soil we grow in and the water we are given. Environment is vitally important. It determines how the seedling will grow and if it will reach maturity and bear fruit. Good environment can be a question of life and death. Let us look at two of the many different environments that have shaped our type.

Parents

The effect of our parents is so profound (or of the people we grew up with in the case where it was not our biological parents) that it is only with great difficulty that we can distinguish their influence from our inborn type. It is important to see this influence in order to decide what we really are in ourselves and how we can develop our own true potential. Our parents imprint their types on us with their good traits and positive energies, as well as their weaknesses and fears. This they do by simply being who they are as our parents and also by having expectations both voiced and unvoiced about what we should be like. In order to map out their influence we have to know what their types are and then see how they have interacted with our own. The following examples will give you some idea of the problems children face that can be explored from the point of view of types.

Peter, an ES father and Sammy, an IU son.

It always upset Peter when he would come home from work or be home for the weekend, and there Sammy would be in his room, reading a book or playing endlessly with his toy soldiers. "What was the matter with that kid? He was so quiet and had just a few friends and was always dreaming and tripping over his own feet. How would he ever amount to anything if he didn't get some get-up-and-go. Why, when I was a kid I played on the Little League ball team, I had dozens of friends, and I had a part-time job after school as well. You couldn't really say anything without the wife somehow butting in and defending him. He is just a mama's boy."

Richard, an ET father and Rosie, an EF daughter

Rosie loved to be out with her friends, especially the Saturday afternoon movies with all the local kids. But when Saturday would roll around, her father would come up with a long list of house-cleaning chores, and she rarely finished in time to go.

Martha, an EF mother and Annie, an IU daughter

Annie, age 10, was coming home from school, and as she approached the house she realized with a sinking feeling that the Bridge Club was having a meeting there. "Oh no. She'll want me to face all those ladies and say hello." Sure enough, even though Annie tried to escape by running up the stairs without anyone seeing her, her mother's voice, with a slight threat in it, said, "Annie, come and say hello to everyone", and then in a whisper, "And be sure to be nice." "Hello", Annie mumbled to the ladies, and then fled again, this time with success.

George, an IT father, and Bob, an ES son

Bob couldn't get his father to understand how important it was to him to join the school's football team. He saw it as the way he could be really popular with his classmates. George, on his part, had never been too interested in group sports, and didn't want to see his son waste a lot of time and energy that could go towards more important things, or have him get hurt.

Jim, an IS father, Harriet an IS mother, and Betty, an IU daughter.

Jim and Harriet had a close marriage and got along with each other very well. They had a nice home, and the children never went without anything. It puzzled them greatly, then, when Betty began to misbehave. She would come up with some outlandish schemes. She would complain about the bedtime hour or not being allowed to go play in the neighbors' yards. When some of the girls on the block were going to summer camp, Betty wanted to go, too, and couldn't understand her parents' refusal. Betty just didn't realize all the trouble that could happen if they let her go off. They were just looking out for her. Why couldn't she understand this? Betty, for her part, could not understand how everything could be so perfect and orderly and organized and she could still be so unhappy.

On the surface, these stories are commonplace and ordinary, and each of us has dozens of them about our own childhood. What possible value could they have in helping us to have a deep insight into ourselves and our relationship with our parents? Let's take our 1st example of Peter and Sammy, and explore it further. Little Sammy's type and his father's can be represented as follows:

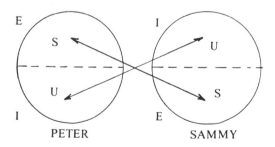

Sammy has a natural weakness in the area of extraverted sensation. This is what is irritating his father to begin with, and his father unwittingly, by making an issue of Sammy's deficiencies, is widening the split between the conscious and the unconscious, or the ES part of Sammy's personality and the rest of it. This just aggravates the problem and will make it more difficult for Sammy to cope with his inferior function, both now and in the future. His father can't really appreciate Sammy's gifts, either, because they strike him at his weakest point, and he unthinkingly perceives them with an aura of suspicion and even potential danger. We tend to sympathize with little Sammy, but his father is not deliberately trying to make trouble for him, and is himself disappointed because he doesn't have the kind of son he wished for. If both of them understood the typological differences involved, they would have a much better chance for a deeper relationship and a more fruitful one.

If the basic outline of our type interaction with our parents is clear, we can begin to explore our personal history in regards to them, especially moments that have high feeling energy. Take an event and see if you can explain it in terms of your type and that of your parents. This kind of procedure can actually release all sorts of energy. Use this energy in a positive, constructive fashion to develop your type. There is little use in blaming your parents for what they did or did not do. What were their parents like? The important point is to break the chain of events in yourself so you do not blindly pass on your own problems to those you influence. If your feelings build up too strongly, back off until you can get them under control or release them in a controlled way in private. Go where you can be alone and do some shouting and crying and beating of pillows about what should have been done and how you should have been treated. Then get on with the job of constructive personal change. We can change ourselves but not change others directly, so most face-to-face recriminations about the past are worse than useless. Resist the sometimes almost irresistible tendency to confront your parents with their apparent shortcomings. We can follow the same sort of procedure with our brothers and sisters and childhood friends and teachers, etc., and see how they shaped us in this early formative period.

Society

The everyday world we live in has its own particular type preferences. Societies differ among themselves, and even change their preferences over time, but each of us has been effected by the type ideas of the particular society we have spent our formative years in. Sheldon felt, as far back as the 1940's, that the United States was in the midst of a mesomorphic revolution that was overturning the ectotonic values of an earlier age. This matched Jung's perception of America being highly extraverted in attitude, and it remains true today that the most popular models held up for imitation in American society are predominantly mesomorphic and extraverted. Naturally, there are many cross-currents and exceptions, but by-and-large we imbibe the extraverted mesomorphic model from our earliest years.

This model is not suitable for other types, and leads to much unnecessary frustration and a sense of failure on their part. It is not even healthy for the people who are mesomorphic and extraverted. It accentuates their already keen sense of competition, and makes it more difficult for them to relax and find the peace and leisure necessary to develop their other side. If we define excellence by who is the winner, it will be limited to the few, while the vast majority of people appear as also-rans. Let us look at several of these models to see this process at work.

One model is the professional athlete. Many young people are encouraged to take part in competitive sports with the idea, often implicit and in the background, but present nonetheless, that everyone has an equal chance to win, and thus move up the ladder towards being some kind of champion. This is the athletic version of American democracy and equal opportunity, but it is based on a false premise. While training and the will to win are vital ingredients in athletic competition, they cannot take the place of an absence of the proper biological equipment. It takes a very particular kind of 90 lb. weakling to turn into Mr. Universe, and it takes a particular kind of obese woman to pose for the before and after pictures in a diet advertisement. All children are not born with the same degree of mesomorphy, and so indiscriminate encouragement of athletic competition among them is going to lead to fore-ordained results. If we continue to think of ectomorphs as underweight and undeveloped mesomorphs, and endomorphs as overweight and lazy mesomorphs, we will continue to demand that they show the same posture and perform the same exercises as the mesomorphs, and this amounts to a kind of body type discrimination. Athletic coaches with extensive experience in selecting people for professional competitive sports have, no doubt, developed instinctive guidelines by which they can select the most likely candidates. Each sport probably has a distinctive area of the somatotype chart from which most of the top-flight competitors come. If the relationship between athletic performance and somatotype would become more conscious, it would be helpful not only in selecting athletic competitors, but in tailoring physical fitness programs for endomorphs and ectomorphs who have a real need of them precisely because they are not instinctively inclined to exercise like the mesomorphs.

Another model held up for emulation in our society is that of the actor or actress, which includes a great deal of the territory of the professional singer. Sheldon felt that acting, far from being a democratic opportunity open to all, demanded a high degree of mesomorphy and extraversion. This is because the actors need to project their voices and feelings, and have a face whose expressions are easily readable by the audience. Our standards of beauty are also highly selective in terms of body type and temperament. The current feminine and masculine ideas of beauty run towards mesomorphy, with a good measure of ectomorphy added. Boys look to their biceps, and girls to their breasts, to gauge how well their development is coming along, but the appearance of our models of beauty is much more a biological gift than it is a product of training. Instead of equating beauty with ectomorphic mesomorphy, we should free ourselves to appreciate the genuine beauty of endomorphs, ectomorphs, and short endomorphic mesomorphs, in other words, of all the somatotypes.

Still another model that is popular in the American scene is that of the hard-driving, self-made, millionaire businessman. Isn't this an area where equal opportunity is open to everyone, and each person has a chance to make it big and become rich? Certainly the physical gifts of the businessman are less apparent than in the case of the athlete or actor, and a wide range of somatotypes and personality types attain business success. But it is probably true that the self-made millionaires tend to share the same body, temperament, and psychological type territories as the other stars of our society. While in the abstract we can all become millionaires, most of us do not possess the physical drive, competitive spirit and single-mindedness that are ingredients of much of the Horatio Alger stories we still hear. The free market is more free for some people than for others.

A final model is that of the politician. Here, again, certain body and temperament types tending towards the mesomorphic and extraverted territories predominate out of proportion to the degree they exist in the general population. It is no accident that athletes become actors and businessmen, and then turn into politicians. It is perhaps inevitable that energetic extraverts will play major public roles, since this is part of their gift. What is unfortunate is that the very word introversion in normal American usage has often obtained a pejorative connotation which did not exist in Jung's original formulation, but was acquired, as if by osmosis, by being brought into an extraverted atmosphere. The extraverted mesomorphic bias in the U.S. proves nothing in itself about the absolute numbers of extraverts or mesomorphs in the country. But it does have important effects on everyone. The non-extraverted, non-mesomorphic personalities are made to feel they are not as successful or adaptive as they should be, while extraverted, mesomorphic personalities are put under greater psychological pressure to compete and perform, which makes more difficult the development of other aspects of their personalities. It is probably true that in certain times in history endotonic and ectotonic models dominated. They were equally one-sided and harmful. What we need are integrated models, even more than a presentation of extreme models. We need to see the whole spectrum of body, temperament and psychological types, and these in their particular processes of development in which they become less one-sided and more in contact with the other dimensions of their own personality.

Types and Falling in Love

Let us return to the question of projection, but this time as found in the process of falling in love. We are not talking about love itself which conquers diversities and binds two different people together in a real union. Falling in love has a dimension of psychological projection that is implicit in the word falling itself, which points to something happening beyond the consciousness of the people involved.

The man projects part of his unconscious self on a suitable woman, while the woman projects part of her unconscious self on the man. The man then sees the woman after the image of the woman within himself and is entranced at finding someone who so closely meets his inner needs. The same happens with the woman if it is a mutual projection. The wonderful feeling of completion that wells up at such a moment springs from the promise of each becoming whole within themselves, but all the while they take it to mean that it is due to having found each other. This phenomenon of projection makes it easier to understand love at first sight when we have no real knowledge of the other person. It also shows why one person can fall in love and the other be unaware of it or indifferent to it.

The projection can be one of the man's feeling function and the woman's thinking function. It could be a projection of sensation and intuition. Jung was of the opinion that a great many marriages were marriages of opposites. The ES type often marries the IU type, the EF type marries the IT type, etc., but less complete kinds of opposites are very common as well. Do they have to do this? Of course not. But the initial attraction is the strongest because the projection is the strongest, and the projection is often strongest among opposites.

The wonderful discovery of just the right person to make ourselves complete is the power of romance and early marriage, but there is no shortcut to real development of the personality. We must become whole within ourselves—to be united with our other side. Soon the married couple can begin to see that the other is not quite what they thought they were, and the magic of the projected image begins to fade away. This can lead to a feeling of being deceived and betrayed by the other, and hard on this feeling follow recriminations and bitterness. The two people are in fact sometimes worlds apart and it would take the best will in the world for them to really understand how the other functions. But instead of the best will there is ill will and hard feelings that throttle understanding at its very inception. This does not mean that two opposite types cannot marry well. But to the degree that they marry under the influence of projections, to that degree they are storing up future difficulties.

John, an ES type, and Susan, an IU type:

Susan could never figure out how John, who had seemed so daring and adventuresome when they were going together, could have turned out to be so routine-bound. It was a major operation to pry him loose from the house whenever it was a question of taking her and the kids out for the day. He was quick enough to go out with his friends two or three times a week if she would let him, but when it came to vacation time it was like pulling teeth to get him to go someplace new and different.

John, for his part, couldn't quite understand why Susan seemed on edge. They had a nice home and a good income, and yet she seemed half overwhelmed with the housework, taking the kids to dancing lessons and all the other chores she took upon herself. She couldn't even seem to get the floor cleaned right, not to mention to get it through her head that when the weekend rolled around, he didn't want it all laid out for a bunch of crazy trips that meant driving halfway across the state when they could enjoy themselves just as well right here. Susan always had a new kick, and was forever dragging books home, but he figured he had to give her time and it would blow over like so many things in the past. It always made him feel uneasy when she hustled the kids into the car and went flying off on some errand. Half the time he was really tempted to go along, just to make sure she got there in one piece, why with all the drunk drivers and wild kids on the road you never knew what was going to happen.

Sam, an IT type, and Helen, an EF type:

Eight years of marriage had left them with 3 children, a lot of bills, and not much feeling left for each other. For Helen, Sam was a wet blanket on any ideas she might have to make her life more pleasant, like bridge at the Harris', art classes at the local college, a backyard b-b-q with the neighbors, or just simply anything.

For Sam, Helen never had a real idea in her head. All she had was some wild notions that she never stopped to weigh or plan out. Long ago he had learned not to commit himself to a project that demanded that he do all the work while she flitted around and posed. The last party they had had was, in his mind, a disaster. He had so many details to look after that he never got a chance to really enjoy the few people out of that whole mob that he felt he could talk to. Let him try to explain a little something about his work at the lab, and what a blank stare he got. Helen often said to her friends, "I wouldn't mind Sam making life miserable for me, but I won't stand for him to make life miserable for the children. How could a man who is supposed to be so smart not realize all the things the kids need and how much money it takes to get them? The kids have to go to the right school and wear the right clothes and entertain their friends once in a while, and these things do cost some money. What does he expect us to do? Sit around grim and silent smoking a pipe?"

Types and Children

Children from their earliest days exhibit distinctive forms of behavior that can be understood in terms of types. Many parents have noticed how different their children are despite their growing up in the same home environment, and as far as the parents can determine, with the same kind of love and affection. While not underestimating the effect of early parental influence, parents can take far too much upon themselves if they think that all the real and deep-seated differences they see in their children result only from their own behavior towards the child. Once the parents realize that the child has its own distinctive personality from birth, then they can see their role in a clearer fashion. There are two people who interact, no matter how unequally, in the parent-child relationship. The viewpoint of the child is not simply something it has picked up from its home environment.

Step-by-step the parents can gain a knowledge of the child's personality type on all three levels. This is a good framework in which to understand the child's strengths and weaknesses. Through it the parents can get a more appropriate idea of what the eating and sleeping habits of the child are according to their type, and the child's need for exercise, quiet time, etc.

The best time to focus on the child's weakness is in early childhood, not in a depreciating, negative manner, but in a positive and constructive reinforcement. It is almost as if the child's strengths will come out as long as they are not actually obstructed, and in this sense it is more important to foster the weakest dimension of the personality. For example, an IU boy with a high verbal ability and lively imagination can find enough stimulation for these talents without a special program of development. There is a natural inclination for society to foster the development of the most differentiated function of the child. This is because the community rates the individual not on their wholeness but on the distinctive contribution each can make to it. Parents often follow this same pattern. They see that a child has a particular gift, and they go out of their way to cultivate that gift, whether it is some kind of artistic or athletic or intellectual ability. The unfortunate result can be a child who develops one-sidedly. It could be argued that the parents' energies would be better spent in developing the weakest side of the child's personality. What would be the impact of the warm family environment in which the inferior function of the child could be nurtured? This, of course, demands a recognition on the part of the parents of their own strengths and weaknesses so that they don't impose them on the child and expect him to excel in areas where they have excelled. The parents have to recognize the nature of the inferior function which is such that no amount of nurturing will make it totally like the more conscious parts of the personality. At the same time, in the right setting, many of the later problems that the inferior function could cause can be smoothed away.

The parents also have a responsibility to monitor the environments in which the child lives outside the home in order to see if there is enough freedom in them for their child's particular kind of developmental needs. There has to be room in the school room, the church activity group, the clubs, the sports teams, for all different types of children. If one model is held up to the exclusion of all others, then many children will be harmed.

The field of adoption is another place where it is important to recognize differences in type. If the couple who wants to adopt a child is aware of their own types and the varying degrees of difficulty with which they deal with other types, they can either look for the type of child that will be compatible with them or be aware that the child, no matter how young they have received it, could have a temperament and psychological type very distinct from their own. For example, an extraverted couple has to be aware of the possibility of adopting an introverted child in order that their own expectations will not be disappointed and that the child will not be put at an immediate disadvantage.

Children, even at 8 or 10 years old, and perhaps even before that, can develop a surprisingly good knowledge of body, temperament and psychological types. It gives them a framework within which their parents can explain countless situations, and the children themselves can begin to make their own tentative explanations. A knowledge of types is a valuable tool in the hands of children, provided their parents can frame suitable explanations as different situations come up.

In the give-and-take of active family life, if all the members of the family are aware of their inferior function, it makes them more tolerant of each other. The children can distinguish bit by bit the occasions when they are being yelled at due to their own misconduct from those in which they have simply rubbed their parents' inferior function the wrong way, and the parents can learn to admit when they are upset because of their own weakness.

Projection and Prejudice

The mechanism of projection is all around us and at the source of many misunderstandings and hatreds. We have talked about it in typological terms, but this is simply one way of approaching the conflicts around us. White America has harsh words and contempt for Blacks, Indians, and Mexican Americans. Yet the dreams of the white men are filled with these people, making it quite clear how much of a projection this racial prejudice is. No doubt the projection works both ways. In a similar manner the West loathes the East and the Arabs hate the Jews, and the Irish the English and on and on without end. The real fire for such hatred is not in historical events which add fuel, but in the lack of integration, and to the degree we fail to come to grips with the full extend of our own personality, we project the unconscious contents outward on those around us. Those contents, since they have been neglected and starved for attention for so long, can be crude and antagonistic, frightening and bestial, which are precisely the characteristics of the classic enemy—whether it be a Communist, white man, red man or whatever.

There is, of course, good and bad actions of individuals and nations, as well as varying levels of culture and different value systems. But we cannot come to grips with these objective issues until we are aware of our own subjective projections which distort all we see like mirrors in the fun house - or should it be the house of horrors. Erich Neumann's *Depth Psychology and the New Ethic* provides an incisive analysis of this kind of projection.

If you know your own type and that of the other person, you are in a position to try to unravel the intricacies of your relationship with him or her. Perhaps the most fruitful place to start is in your family and the people closest to you. Take one relationship and try to see how much mutual projection there has been and where it has come from. Just this much understanding will be a giant step in alleviating conflicts. The enduring remedy, however, is the full development of your own type.

Part III
The Future of Typology

Chapter 7

Toward a Science
of Human Differences

In Part I we were concerned with the simple introduction of Jung's and Sheldon's typologies and how they can be brought together. In Part II we considered some of the uses of such a united typology within the framework of Jung's process of individuation.

Part III is a series of reflections and speculations on some of the important problems that stand in the way of the development of a science of human differences that would be useful not only for professional psychologists, psychiatrists, counselors, etc., but for everyone. This chapter is concerned with the question of the different ways of doing science which is at the bottom of divergent tendencies in the study of Jungian typology and in the field of human differences in general. This critical theoretical issue has a very practical corollary in the form of what could be called the diagnostic question. How can a sure estimation of type be arrived at?

Chapter 8 considers some of the ways in which evidence can be generated in favor of the relationship between somatotype and psychological type. Chapter 9 goes on to examine some of the implications of this relationship and the possible applications of this unified typology to other fields. Finally, we engage in some tentative speculations about the genetic basis to psychological types.

Each one of these topics could be the subject of a whole volume. Hopefully, their presentation here in summary form will be a first step towards their more complete elaboration, which is a work that belongs to the future of typology.

The Genesis of *Psychological Types*

An examination of the origin of Jung's *Psychological Types* can help us to understand not only how *Psychological Types* came to be published in 1921, but something about the development of typology since that time, and its possibilities for the future. C. A. Meier, who was closely associated with Jung from 1924, provides a valuable guide to this area in his *Psychological Types and Individuation* (1971).

The formal beginning of Jung's types, though it had earlier antecedents in his word association experiments, can be placed at Munich in September of 1913 when Jung delivered a paper to the 4th International Psychoanalytic Congress entitled, *"A Contribution to the Study of Psychological Types."* It described the nature of extraversion and introversion and the need of psychology to take into account these distinctively different viewpoints. It represented the beginning of Jung's open break with Freud; they never met again after this time. The paper was a definitive step by which Jung attempted to distinguish his own viewpoint from that of the founder of the psychoanalytic movement.

Later in the fall of 1913 Jung asked himself, "What is your myth by which you live?" and he had no answer. He stopped lecturing at the University of Zurich in order to focus on this question, and he leaves us the exact date of Dec. 12, 1913 when he gathered up his courage and resolve and took the decisive step to go down into the inner world of the unconscious on a voyage of self-discovery. He was 38 years old, and this adventure was to last until 1918-19.

There are two interwoven strands to the development of *Psychological Types*. One is interpersonal where Jung distinguished his own point of view, and the other is intrapsychic, where he confronted the unconscious. In the next few years both elements contributed to the elaboration of psychological types. Jung did not work on the structure of his typology alone, but collaborated with a number of people. For example, his initial identification of introversion with thinking and extraversion with feeling was clarified by his correspondence with Dr. Hans Schmid during 1915-16.

On the interior plane Jung was going through what he was later to call the process of individuation. And he was going through it alone without chart or guide. In fact, he was creating his compass in terms of *Psychological Types* as he went, and using it to map out the inner journey that led to the self. He had painted his first mandala in 1916 but had not understood it. It was not until 1918-19 he began to grasp the central meaning of the self. He says:

> During those years between 1918 and 1920 I began to understand the goal of psychic development is the self... This insight gave me stability and gradually my inner peace returned. I knew that in finding the mandala as an expression of the self I had attained what for me was the ultimate. (1961, p. 196-197)

Even the emergence from the confrontation with the unconscious had an exterior dimension. Jung broke with a woman who was determined that he should give his interior fantasies an artistic meaning.

When the massive volume of *Psychological Types* appeared, it was hardly the question of a miraculous birth. Jung's own process of individuation was the fiery magma out of which developed all his later work, and the first major crystallization out of this matrix was his work on types. Therefore it is not surprising to find there a chapter where he defines his basic terms, nor to find the first use of the term *the self*. When H.G. Baynes translated the book into English in 1923 bearing the subtitle *The Psychology of Individuation*, this was no exaggeration. *Psychological Types* represents his first major attempt to delineate the individuation process, and as such it bears traces of Jung's own personal development, Chapter 2, *"Schiller's Ideas on the Type Problem"*, deals with the *"typical conflict of the Introverted Thinking Type"* which Jung felt himself to be. This is the most probable reason why he had originally equated introversion with thinking and extraversion with feeling. The point to note is the personal roots *Psychological Types* had both intrapsychically and interpsychically. Jung in complete earnestness tries to make this clear at the very beginning of the *Forward to the First Swiss Edition*:

> This book is the fruit of nearly twenty years' work in the domain of practical psychology. It grew gradually in my thoughts, taking shape from the countless impressions and experiences of a psychiatrist in the treatment of nervous illnesses, from the intercourse with men and women of all social levels, from my

personal dealings with friend and foe alike, and finally from a critique of my own personal psychological peculiarity. (1921, p. xi.)

Under these conditions Jung must have certainly wished for a warm reception for his first-born child. What he got instead was summed up by Spittler's reaction, whose *Prometheus and Epimetheus* featured largely in what Jung felt to be a critical chapter, *"The Type Problem in Poetry."* Jung states:

> I was presumptuous enough to send a copy of my book to Spittler. He did not answer me, but shortly afterward delivered a lecture in which he declared positively that his *Prometheus and Epimetheus* 'meant' nothing, that he might just as well have sung 'Spring is come, tra-la-la-la.' (1961, p. 207)

There were exceptions, of course, but the reception by Jung's peers was hardly encouraging. Jung felt unjustly accused of having invented psychological types as a kind of intellectual parlor game, and then using it to stick superficial labels on people. This continued to bother him for a long time. Fourteen years later he says:

> ... it is not the case at all that I begin by classifying my patients into types and then give them the corresponding advice as a colleague of mine whom God has endowed with a peculiar wit once asserted. (Letters, v. 1, p. 186)

In a similar fashion, in the *Forward to the Argentine Edition*, he emphasizes the need for the reader to immerse himself in Chapters II and V: "He will gain more from them than from any typological terminology superficially picked up, since this serves no other purpose than a totally useless desire to stick on labels."

If the impact of *Psychological Types* was not exactly earthshaking on the professional circles Jung had addressed himself to, it did have an influence on a wider audience of people who were not psychiatrists and psychoanalysts. The terms extraversion and introversion came into general use, and psychologists took them up and attempted to create instruments to measure them. Katherine Briggs and her daughter Isabel Briggs-Myers were inspired to use Jung's Typology as the basis for a long study of the subject that gave birth to the Myers-Briggs

Type Inaicator many years later. James Oppenheim, who worked for a time as a Jungian analyst in the United States, wrote a book which appeared in 1929 entitled *American Types*. This book tried to put types in an American perspective and, interestingly enough, made an attempt to develop a physiognomy of the types based on an equation of facial features with Jung's typology.

There were two somewhat distinct audiences, then, that appreciated Jung's typology from the beginning. One was made up of his collaborators and the other was a more general audience which included not only professional psychologists but many of the ordinary readers Jung liked to point to who read and appreciated, not to mention bought, his books. But this audience did not have the same background and preoccupations as that of the professional analyst. They tended to look at it more from an interpersonal than an intrapsychic point of view. They began to wonder how types could be made easier, be measured by psychological tests, be applied to the question of vocational choices, etc.

This was not an approach that coincided with Jung's own predilection. His own inner process of discovery centered on the intrapsychic dimension of types as an expression of the process of individuation, and though he used types to help explain to his patients their conflicts with their wives and children, it was always within the analytic situation. In a certain sense, he did not even have to mention types in order to be faithful to his conception of them. He centered his attention on the process of individuation, and this in his mind was a continuation of typology. Then, too, the psychotherapeutic situation with its emphasis on treating mental illness and the difficulty of using typology in an interpersonal way when the neuroticism of the patient throws up material from all parts of the personality, all had an effect on the use of typology as an explicit tool in analysis.

These factors help to explain the wide variance of use of typology in professional Jungian circles. There are those who see it playing a crucial role in the analytic process, while in contrast there are a number of Jungian analysts who make hardly any use of it at all. It is certainly possible to help someone undergo the process of individuation in the analytic situation without the analyst or the analysand averting to their types. Whether it is the ideal situation is, of course, another question. C. A. Meier (1971) and C. Jess Groesbeck (1978) argue convincingly for the important role that types can play in the analytic situation, while A. Plaut (1972) and K. Bradway and W. Detloff (1975) explore the actual use of typology among Jungian analysts. In any event, types are implicit in the analytic process, just as the inferior function is implicit in the confrontation with the unconscious.

Outside professional Jungian circles circumstances dictate a focus on the interpersonal nature of types. This kind of accent is legitimate. We have seen the interpersonal developments that went on in the formulation of types, and the fact that Jung used them interpersonally as well. But there is a danger that the urge of classification, which in itself is good, will lose sight of its foundation in the intrapsychic nature of typology, or in other words, the process of individuation. The treatment of types interpersonally tends to emphasize consciousness and the need of the auxiliary function to strengthen the superior one, and thus achieve a kind of balance. But this balance is quite a different matter than the balance produced by the self. The danger is that this first kind of integration of consciousness will be seen as the ordinary man's individuation, instead of seeing that wholeness and balance for everyone is a question of the relationship of the conscious to the unconscious. In the analytic context there is a real and necessary concern with illness as well as health. The analyst must evaluate the potential danger the analytic process poses for the patient, especially in terms of latent psychosis. In discussing the dangers that face someone trying to go through a process of individuation Jung states that the most serious danger:

> is that the subliminal contents already possess such a high energy charge that when afforded an outlet by active imagination they may overpower the conscious mind and take possession of the personality. (1916/1957, p. 68)

This is the perspective in which he considers the question of lay analysis and says further of active imagination: "The method, therefore, is not without its dangers and should, if possible, not be employed except under expert supervision." (1916/1957, p. 68)

This is certainly a far different situation from administering a psychological type test, scoring the results and then discussing with the test-taker his agreement with the type indicated and some of the practical applications it can have on school work, vocational choice, etc. This is typology as many people are now being introduced to it. The real question is not the legitimacy of using types in these two highly divergent ways, but whether this divergence will widen. Typology cannot afford to be split according to the intra and inter psychic. This kind of split is too reminiscent of the split between the types that typology is trying to resolve in the first place. Without close attention to the intrapsychic dimension of types and the individuation process, the use of types as a means of interpersonal classification will lose its moorings and be in danger of becoming a facile system of labeling that Jung so feared. From another perspective, with the best will in the world, the small group of Jungian analysts cannot deal single-handedly within the analytic temenos with all the people who would profit greatly from typological knowledge. If Jung's typology is going to get the widespread attention it deserves, new ways of propagating it are necessary. At a deeper level, if the process of individuation is a central process of human psychic development, then it, too, must in some fashion be brought to a wider audience in an effective way outside of the analytic situation. Impossible? No. Extremely difficult? Yes. Typology is one of the best ways in which to do this, for it represents a certain visibility of the individuation process. The exposition of typology must avoid getting people in over their heads, while at the same time giving them the tools to work on the process of individuation which is the best hope for a solution to their interpersonal problems.

Two Conceptions of Psychological Science

The differences in approach found within Jungian typology could be viewed as reflections of the wider divergences in method that exist in the field of human differences in general. Jung, and Sheldon working out of the tradition of Kretschmer, both had medical backgrounds and relied heavily on personal contact and observation in order to discover the empirical facts upon which they based their typologies. Their methodology contrasts markedly with that of the factor analysis school, which has also done extensive work in the field of extraversion and introversion, as well as somatotypes. Here the conception of science is based more rigorously on models derived from the physical sciences like chemistry and physics. Initial data is gathered through experimentation by a variety of techniques such as direct physical measurement and standardized written tests, and then it is submitted to mathematical analysis. This process yields more general factors which can explain the data and give rise to further experimentation.

Jung conceived of his way of doing science somewhat differently. He based himself on the evidence of empirical facts, but he felt that evidence varied in kind from discipline to discipline. A fact in psychology, while it had to be empirical, i.e., observable, was not necessarily measurable by exact physical means: "The more we turn from spacial phenomena to the non-spaciality of the psyche, the more impossible it becomes to determine anything by exact physical measurement." (1931, p. 527). Nor could it be always determined by experimental means, for an experiment, he felt, imposed conditions on the psyche, and thus limited the range of the psyche's possible responses. He says:

> Experiment, however, consists in asking a definite question which excludes as far as possible anything disturbing and irrelevant. It makes conditions, imposes them on Nature, and in this way forces her to give an answer to a question devised by man. She is prevented from answering out of the fullness of her possibilities since these possibilities are restricted as far as practicable. (1952, p. 451).

Do we have to choose between these two conceptions of science? Do we have to label Jung's approach as subjective, by which is meant irrational, and write him off as a myth-maker and mystic? Or if we appreciate his way of proceeding, is it necessary to disparage the other approaches as materialistic and soul-deadening, and better fit for mice than men? Such a choice would not only be superficial but damaging in the long run to the development of a viable science of human differences. If we eliminated the work of Sheldon and Jung, and its influence, and even its ability to evoke counter responses, the field of human differences would be much poorer for it. If we were to ignore the work of other schools, we would also seriously impoverish this embryonic science. Both approaches can stimulate and even provoke each other to new insights. How much really significant development has taken place in Jung's typology since the publication of *Psychological Types*? How much work has been done to bring it into relationship with other scientific disciplines? Not nearly enough. On the other hand, while an extensive literature is growing up around the concepts of extraversion, introversion and somatotypes, it often ignores Jung and Sheldon and is less significant for it. For example, Jung, after his initial presentation of extraversion and introversion in 1913, had serious second thoughts about this whole conception, because wider experience convinced him that it was inadequate. He then embarked on what he considered a long and difficult process to refine this initial conception in terms of the various kinds of introversion and extraversion, that is, in terms of the four functions. Unfortunately, this refinement has been virtually ignored outside of Jungian circles. Are we to imagine that Jung, who had so much to say about introversion and extraversion, which has proved accurate, was totally mistaken about his definitive way of conceiving these two attitudes? This is an area that could be fruitfully explored by other schools in the same way they have worked on the two basic attitudes.

The two conceptions of the science of human differences can be viewed as complementary. If we read, for example, the three-volume collection of articles, *Readings in Introversion and Extraversion,* edited by H. J. Eysenck, there are many points that are convergent with insights drawn on the work of Sheldon and Jung. These include the higher sedation thresholds of introverts, and their lower auditory and pain thresholds (Laverty, 1958; Smith, 1968) and the higher pain tolerance of extraverts. (Lynn and Eysenck, 1961). There have been studies since that time which are of great interest for a better appreciation and extension of the work of Jung and Sheldon, for example, the relationship between the AB blood group and introversion (Eysenck, 1982), the retention of radioactive iodine by ectomorphs (Dubey et al. 1978), and others. What prevents a closer working relationship between the Jungian school, the followers of Sheldon, and the factor analysis school is chiefly the unresolved questions about the different conception of science involved. This conflict is part of the essential background in which to view the criticisms leveled against Sheldon's work. Which conception of science did Sheldon follow? At first glance he appears to be employing exact measurement and mathematical analysis, but this is misleading. Without trying to decide about the accuracy of his mathematical techniques, we feel he is best understood when he is placed in Jung's company in terms of scientific methodology. L. L. Thurstone gives us an interesting criterion for trying to clarify this point, when in a talk to the Psychometric Society in 1936 on the establishment of psychology as a quantitative and rational science, he distinguishes the use of mathematics as an aid or tool from its use as the very language in which the psychologist thinks. No one would make the mistake of imagining that Jung thought in the language of mathematics, and while Sheldon used mathematics, a case could be made that he did not think in the language of mathematics. For example, even though he worked with Thurstone on his original attempt to mathematically represent his constitutional conclusions, they were not to find favor with later factor analysis advocates. Further, Sheldon was apparently in no rush to try to objectify his somatotyping procedures. He moved from observation to measurement and back again. It was only with the urging from his long-standing associates Eugene McDermott and C. Wesley Dupertuis, that he produced his final objective method.

A balanced presentation of Sheldon's work and the criticism of it can be found in Hall and Lindzey in their second edition of *Theories of Personality*. Two points are essential if Sheldon's work is to be properly evaluated. The first is his final metric procedure of somatotyping which we will touch on later, and the second and deeper problem is the two conceptions of science. Figure 5 represents one way of visualizing this problem.

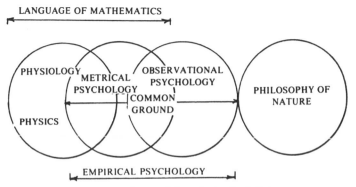

Fig. 5. Two Conceptions of Psychological Science.

The factor analysis school is attracted to the physical sciences and physiology, and the mathematical interpretation of the data they accumulate, as well as the creation of biological hypotheses about the nature of introversion and extraversion. (Eysenck, 1967). Jung and Sheldon, while engaged in a detailed study of empirical facts, and while legitimately staying within the field of psychology, were attracted in another direction. Jung, while trying to maintain his scientific stance, was drawn over and over again to philosophical and religious questions which he attempted to treat from a psychological point of view. Sheldon wrote his first and last books about what he felt were religious questions.

An understanding of the methodology used by Jung and Sheldon can help us appreciate the relatively wide-spread recognition and use their work received. It was not because they eschewed strict scientific methodology and wrote in a popular vein, but rather their typological hypotheses were conceptualizable by people outside their own immediate fields. They spoke to the individual experience and conceptual imagination of their readers, most of whom were not drawn to a strictly mathematical approach.

Although Jung created a technical vocabulary and used words like *soul* and *psychic energy* which took on a particular psychological meaning, the nonprofessional reader could attempt to understand these formulations by analogy with his own experience. This is even more true in the case of Sheldon whose descriptions of the basic components of physique coined new words, but related them to basic anatomical facts. The mathematical treatment of psychological data, however, often produces a conception of man which is not readily understandable in terms of personal experience. The nonprofessional reader has a much more difficult task in applying the results of these kinds of studies to his own particular case. As Allport stated:

> The factors thus obtained represent only *average* tendencies. Whether a factor is really an *organic* disposition in any one individual life is not demonstrated. All one can say for certain is that a factor is an empirically derived component of the *average* personality, and that the average personality is a complete abstraction. This objection gains point when one reflects that seldom do the factors derived in this way resemble the dispositions and traits identified by clinical methods when the individual is studied intensively. (1937, p. 244).

Even though a case can be made, for example, for the accuracy of written testing to determine the percentage of type in a large sample--as we will do in Chapter 8--this is no guarantee of the accuracy of the test individual by individual, which, of course, is critical for personal therapy.

The resolution of this conflict does not lie in the direction of denying the scientific validity of either approach. Rather, it is to be found in a more flexible and nuanced interpretation of science which can allow for varied methods even when dealing with the same subject matter. What is needed is a noetic or epistemological typology that allows individual differences to exist, in this case specific scientific methodologies within a common scientific framework. Jacques Maritain (1959) sheds valuable light on this matter in his analysis of the modern sciences when he distinguishes between what he calls the empiriometrical sciences and the empirioschematic. The former, which include theoretical physics and a factor analytic approach to somatotypes and psychological types, start from empirical data, i.e., the sensible real, and ultimately find their verification there, but are formally mathematical. The empirioschematic sciences, which would include Sheldon's and Jung's psychologies, while still based on the sensible real, and while maintaining their autonomy according to principles, method and conceptual vocabulary, have a certain affinity towards the philosophy of nature. The different conceptual vocabularies used in each case preclude direct comparisons of, for example, a mathematical approach to somatotypes to Sheldon's work. In the next volume of *The Tools for Inner Growth* series we will treat some of these epistemological questions at greater length.

The Diagnosis of Somatotype

The diagnostic question represents the extension of the problem of scientific methodology into the practical realm. Somatotype can be established by a variety of methods whose range illustrates the two conceptions of science and their interrelationship. (For the sake of simplicity, we will not examine the variants on Sheldon's methods that Parnell, Heath and Carter have devised. For a comparison of these methods with Sheldon's, cf., Villanueva, 1979). The chief methods are:

115

1. Structured Observation. A knowledge of the height and weight history of the subject, and the charts provided in *The Atlas of Men*, lead to the selection of the most probable somatotypes. The final determination of somatotype is done by comparison with the pictures in *The Atlas of Men*. Dr. Sheldon employed this method using standardized nude photographs. It can also be used without formal somatotype photographs as a simple process of evaluation by observation, though, of course, with less accuracy.

2. The Trunk Index Method. This was Sheldon's last and most objective method based on height, maximum weight and the determination of the Trunk Index, which is the ratio of the chest to the abdominal area, taken with a planimeter from a standardized somatotype photograph. Sheldon provided detailed tables to convert this data into the somatotype number. He felt that the Trunk Index was stable during weight change, muscular development and growth over long periods of time, and that this method answered the chief criticisms brought against his work: that the somatotype changes, is not objective, consists of only two primary components, and omits the factor of size. (1969, pp. 848-849).

3. The Structural Profile and the Shape Index. Developed by C. Wesley and Helen S. Dupertuis (1974), clinical anthropologists and long-time associates of Dr. Sheldon, the as yet unpublished Structural Profile is based on 11 skeletal measurements representing all the major areas of the body, and height and weight. With 3 additional measurements, a skeletal version of Sheldon's Trunk Index, called the Shape Index, can be determined which highly correlates with it and remains constant over time. The Structural Profile provides a metrical method for determining somatotype without the use of photography, as well as additional valuable information not available from the Trunk Index method alone.

There is a movement from observation to measurement in Sheldon's work, and he was aware that the process of somatotyping should gradually become more and more metrical, but the actual process was not a simple one. His arrangement of his initial series of 4,000 somatotype photographs was by observation. Later, he quantified this procedure by the use of 17 measurements, plus height and weight, and showed it yielded comparable results. This quantification was limited to college-age males, and in subsequent work Sheldon devised the method of structured observation which had a much wider range of application and was quicker and easier to use. Still later, he developed the Trunk Index method. The Trunk Index differentiated between endomorphy and mesomorphy, while height became the gauge of ectomorphy.

These alternations of method allow us to look at the two conceptions of science at the level of practical diagnosis. They formed two aspects of the one exploratory process by which Sheldon delved deeper into the questions of somatotypes. Without observation, the metrical methods would never have developed, and without the metrical methods, the observations would not have reached final fruition. Retrospectively, Sheldon felt that his final metrical method vindicated his earlier observational ones by showing that the results from both procedures were fairly close. Even at a relatively early stage of his career, at the time of the writing of *The Varieties of Temperament*, Sheldon was concerned with the validity of the observational method. He conducted several experiments in which the ratings of relatively untrained observers, as well as highly trained observers, were compared to the results obtained by objective somatotpying. (Tables 17 and 18, *The Varieties of Temperament.*) The results indicated a high degree of agreement between the anthropometric and the observational method.

Walker and Tanner (1980), in a study of the predictability of the adult somatotype, employed both the anthroposcopic and the Trunk Index methods. They found interjudged correlations for the anthroposcopic ratings ranging from .79-.93, while the correlations for the Trunk Index method ranged from .94-.99. The mean somatotype changed little with age by either method, and the correlations between the two ratings were in the low .80s. In the case of the anthroposcopic ratings, nearly 40% of the ratings were identical, and nearly 80% within a half point. With the Trunk Index method, there was nearly complete agreement for ectomorphy, and 87-96% of the ratings for mesomorphy and endomorphy fell within a half a point.

It would be an oversimplification to treat the three methods of somatotyping as three ways to reach identical results. The situation is more complex than this, and there are nuances between the variables that each method uncovers. Walker and

Tanner point this out in connection with the Trunk Index and anthroposcopic methods. It is no doubt true, as well, when the Trunk Index is determined by skeletal measurements, as is the case in using the Shape Index. Why the differences arise and the implications they have for the use of the different methods in different applications is only slowly being explored. The amount of work that compares the use of two methods remains small (Livson and McNeil, 1962; Walker, 1978 and Hartl, Monnelly and Elderkin, 1982). Since there is not an identity among the results of the different methods, it remains an open question which would be most useful in our present application of relating somatotypes and psychological types. We tend to favor the anthroposcopic because of its easy employment and its consideration of the whole body. Yet, the use of the Trunk Index method may be preferable in the kinds of more rigorous experimentation discussed in chapter 8 which will have to be undertaken to clarify exactly where the division lines fall on the somatotype chart for the psychological type territories, and whether or not there is overlapping.

The convergence of results from the Trunk Index and the anthroposcopic methods can be taken as a confirmation of the general validity of the anthroposcopic method, and this has important practical consequences. While in certain cases metrical methods are to be preferred, there are situations where circumstances dictate the use of observation alone. The method of observation can validly be employed in these situations, and if conflicting estimations arise, they can be resolved by the more metrical methods. What makes observational methods even more acceptable when it is a question of determining the somatotype in relationship to the psychological type is that Sheldon's 267 somatotypes are being divided into only 7 psychological type territories. The determination of these territories relies, for the most part, on the accurate rating of the relative predominance of the three components. Structured observation can provide this degree of accuracy with little difficulty.

The diagnostic question at the level of somatotype is resolvable because of the existence of the metrical methods, and they are made possible by the fact that what is being measured is a physical three-dimensional object. The difficulty that attended the development of the objective methods is a sign of the even more complex problems that have to be faced in the diagnosis of temperament and psychological type. The fact that quantification is now possible in somatotyping should not obscure the underlying principle that both observation and metrical methods can reach the same goal, for observation has to be employed at the level of temperament and psychological type where metrical measurement is not possible in the same way.

The Diagnostic Problem in Relationship to Temperament and Psychological Type

When Sheldon did his initial work in relating temperament to somatotype, though he tried to quantify temperament, he proceeded by way of interviews and observations, spread over a year. He found a high correlation between somatotype and temperament, and even though he had established the temperament ratings before doing the somatotypes, his work was criticized on the grounds that he had done both ratings. He had established the temperament index by observation, laying himself open to the charge that he already could tell what the somatotype was and thus make the temperament fit it, albeit unconsciously. His rejoinder was how could he be expected to determine the temperament without observing the person? He felt that the less contact he had with the subjects, the less chance he had of truly establishing their temperaments. He reports in *The Varieties of Temperament* on various attempts to come to grips with this problem. In one experiment he compared his own ratings of temperament of a class with that of class members rating each other, and in another, he compared his evaluation of temperament, derived from a one-hour interview, with the evaluation of a psychiatrist who had a slightly longer contact with the subjects. In both instances, the results indicated that different observers could agree fairly closely in their evaluation of temperament.

There have been a number of attempts to repeat Sheldon's work on the relationship between somatotype and temperament by means of purely objective methods. Hall and Lindzey (1970) provide a summary of some of these studies. The results in most of them are in the direction that Sheldon indicated, but without finding the high correlations that emerge from his work. In another study, Cortes and Gatti (1965) devised a short self-administered quiz in order to establish the temperament, and used Parnell's method of somatotyping which relies on actual body measurements. In this way, they avoided any criticism of rater-bias. Their results fell short of those obtained by Sheldon in his year-long study. They did, however, come closer to the results Sheldon obtained when he made an initial short evaluation of the subjects of his more detailed study. The magnitude of the correlations found between somatotype and temperament by Cortes and Gatti for very extreme types actually exceed the correlations found by Sheldon using the short forms. An alternative interpretation to the charge of Sheldon's rater-bias is the not unreasonable supposition that Cortes and Gatti's five-minute self-description quiz is not as accurate as Sheldon's year-long series of interviews and observations. If we do not a priori deny the validity of observation, the various degrees of correlation can be seen as reflections of a process of temperament determination that has different levels of refinement. Observation, based on an individual judgment, should not automatically be excluded as a way of establishing an empirical fact. These same facts can be verified by other observers, and two or more people, observing the same fact independently, create no more obstacles to the credibility of that fact than the use of written tests.

At the level of psychological type, we find the same tension between observation and measurement. There are two ways in which type is being established today: observation and psychological type tests. The first approach is open to the accusation of being subjective, especially when supposedly trained people disagree about typological diagnosis. The use of a written test is attractive because it appears to avoid this kind of problem, but it has its difficulties as well. In its origin and initial validation, the test drew heavily on observation and informed judgments. More importantly, it has a difficult task to perform because of the different levels of complexity that exist in the diagnosis of the psychological type. The easiest determination is probably that of extraversion-introversion. At a slightly more difficult level is the judgment of which function of each pair, i.e., thinking-feeling or sensation-intuition, is predominant. A written test might be able to determine these first two questions with a fair degree of accuracy, but the third level of complexity is much more difficult to make a judgment about. This is the question of what function is the primary one, and which is the auxiliary. It is here that questions about stages of development, creativity, and neurosis, as well as parental and environmental overlays, make themselves most felt. Since the person being typed contains both attitudes and all four functions, varying circumstances can bring a function to the foreground and make it appear as if it is the main function, when in fact it is not. Therefore, even though a written test has correctly indicated the predominant attitude and the two predominant functions, it faces a much more difficult task in cutting through the surface manifestation of these functions and determining the order of the functions among themselves. This is the principle reason for not simply administering a psychological type test and immediately trying to use the results without verifying them by a knowledge of the person involved and his own self report.

Testing and observation by an experienced diagnostician should go together in order to accurately determine type. There are several principles that will aid successful diagnosis.

1. An intimate working knowledge of one's own type. This means not simply an accurate knowledge of what our type is, but the inner implications of this knowledge in terms of how it expresses itself in the myriad of details of our daily behavior, and especially how our inferior function, as well as the undeveloped aspects of the other functions, influence our conduct towards other people. Without a knowledge of our personal mechanisms of projection, how can we avoid them?

2. An extensive knowledge of the practical peculiarities of different types. This is an appreciation of the nuances and qualities that affect the function, not only when we consider whether it is introverted or extraverted, but the qualities it manifests in each of the four positions.

3. The use of a psychological type test, or a structured typological interview, to help objectify the observations and get a basic reading on the various predominances.

4. A dialogue with the client about what he considers his psychological type to be. Naturally the weight given to this self report will vary with the degree that the client is informed about

types. The individual who has just been introduced to this area can hardly be expected to render a definitive judgment that will bind himself and everyone else. In most situations where the knowledge of type is to be the starting point for a process of self-development, even if an initial quick diagnosis is correct, it lacks the practical efficacious certitude that comes from a slower and more thorough process of typological discovery.

Since this way of typological diagnosis does rely on observation, it is well to reflect on the subjective qualities of the kind of observation we are talking about. Sometimes it is enlightening and enjoyable to think of Jung and Sheldon as human naturalists--enthusiastic bird watchers of the human species. They were both intensely curious; Sheldon could ride the New York subway system and find sights that, as he says, would keep a somatotologist warm on a winter's night, and Jung could pore through an obscure alchemistic treatise with the inner expectation that it could help unravel the very difficulties he was faced with in the consulting room. They both were immensely experienced in what they did, and experience cannot be facilely discounted. There is a certain amount of truth in saying that a typologist must learn his art, just as the bird watchers, trackers, and other naturalists must learn theirs. Sheldon used to illustrate this point by examples drawn from stock judging, wine-tasting and other areas where so-called subjective judgment had to be accurate enough to base business decisions on.

Sheldon, who spent many hours interviewing his initial subjects for temperament evaluation, later devised shorter tests and structured interviews described in the *Varieties of Temperament*, and could reach a diagnosis much more quickly. Speed came with extensive experience, and it is similar to diagnosis in physical medicine. The first independent diagnosis takes years in terms of medical training, but a widely experienced clinician can be remarkably astute and often rapid as well.

What this amounts to is that although Jung's psychological types are based on empirical material, and what one person has observed can be observed by another, it takes a certain amount of experience to properly evaluate the implications of the empirical material for the actual type diagnosis. One consequence of the diagnostic question should not be overlooked. The practical difficulty of making a psychological type diagnosis has given rise to a tendency to reformulate Jung's typology in order to solve the diagnostic question. Jung never claimed that psychological types was anything more than a scientific hypothesis, so from that point of view there is no reason to believe that it cannot progress and develop and mature as greater experience with the underlying empirical facts accumulates, but if the tendency to reformulate Jung's typology is principally motivated by making it more applicable in the area of the relationship between people of different types, there is a real danger in overlooking the implications that these reformulations have for typology considered in relationship to the process of individuation and the reconciliation of opposites in the personality. If, for example, the inferior function is not conceived as the opposite of the superior function, then it is hard to see why it could not eventually develop as much as the 2nd or 3rd functions, or even the 1st. The polarity of the functions is but one manifestation of the polarity of psychic energy between the conscious and the unconscious that is at the heart of the individuation process. If we change the role of the inferior function, the rest of the dynamics of psychic energy begin to unravel as well.

Typological diagnosis, integrally considered at the three levels of type, instead of becoming a more complex procedure, is actually easier once the initial skills have been gained. What makes it easier is that a wider range of empirical material is available for observation. What is striking in one case may be absent in another, making set rules often difficult to follow. For example, an extreme ectomorphic physique is naturally more suggestive than when it is a question of a midrange somatotype. In other cases, temperamental traits might be in the forefront, like the booming voice of mesotonia or the special kind of amiability of the endotonic. At the level of psychological type, the inferior function might catch a person's attention, or the degree of introversion and extraversion, or even something subtler like the distinctive quality of thinking as a 3rd function. Characteristics from all three levels give rise to particular lines of inquiry, and since there are more roads leading to the final diagnosis, it is often easier. The multiple directions of approach tend to check and confirm each other, yielding a greater certitude.

If somatotypes and temperament types can be brought into relationship with psychological types, then the diagnostic problems present at each level will be mitigated. It is to the question of the ways of establishing such a relationship that we must now turn.

Chapter 8

Concerning the Evidence
for a Relationship Between
Somatotype and Psychological Type

The basic hypothesis that we are examining is whether Jung's typology, considered in its full development, can be integrated with Sheldon's somatotypes and temperament index. Since this is a rather sweeping assertion, it is well to balance it with a more modest goal for this chapter. We will examine a number of lines of reasoning that converge towards the conclusion that such a hypothesis is not only thinkable, but probable, and worth looking into.

Jung, Sheldon and Somatotypes

First, it is useful to examine briefly what Jung thought about the relationship between his psychological types and body types. Basically he felt his prime role was in upholding the sovereignty of the psyche against the materialism of the 19th century and its view of the mind as the epiphenomenon of the brain, and we may assume that this attitude, as well as the reception *Psychological Types* received, did not predispose him to explore this area. Such exploration, Jung felt, would be a difficult endeavor because of the diagnostic problem, but he left the question open, and foresaw its theoretical possibility:

"I personally have the impression that some of Kretschmer's main types are not so far removed from certain of the basic psychological types I have enumerated. It is conceivable that at these points a bridge might be established between the physiological constitution and the psychological attitude. That this has not been done already may be due to the fact that the physiological findings are still very recent while, on the other hand, investigation from the psychological side is very much more difficult, and therefore less easy to understand." (1929, p. 108).

C. A. Meier (1983) felt Jung did not try to build this bridge because Kretschmer's typology was based on somatic phenomena. During Meier's long association with Jung neither Kretschmer nor Sheldon were mentioned.

It is not unreasonable to look at Sheldon's work as a consolidation and clarification of Kretschmer's. It was during a visit to Kretschmer's clinic that he conceived the possibility of taking Kretschmer's psychiatric descriptions and reducing them to basic components and quantifying them. We believe that Sheldon makes possible the bridge between physiological constitution and psychological types that Jung foresaw. Sheldon in 1934-35 not only visited Kretschmer, but spent time in Zurich with Jung. He was, however, preoccupied with the idea of somatotypes at the time, and in later years expressed regret he had not gotten closer to Jung's thought.

Humphrey Osmond (1983) throws valuable light on the relationship between Jung and Sheldon:

"Before I left for Zurich Bill Sheldon gave me a copy of his *Atlas of Men* inscribed to Jung from his former pupil. He told me that he was apologizing to Jung for not having paid sufficient attention to Jung's teachings but explained that he was preoccupied with what was to become somatotyping. When I reached Jung's villa in Kusnacht (the date was November 1955) I carried the *Atlas of Men*. Jung was delighted and said, ' "Why we must always give the body its due—did not your Shakespeare say 'Let me have men around me that are fat, sleek headed men and such as sleep o'nights. Your Cassius has a lean and hungry look, he thinks too much, such men are dangerous.' "
So Jung certainly knew of Sheldon's work and expressed his explicit approval to me and told me to thank Sheldon and give him his congratulation and warm regards."

In summary, Jung and Sheldon were acquainted, and even though neither one, as far as we know, tried to formally relate the two typologies, they probably would not have been surprised if there were a relationship.

An interesting footnote to Jung's attitude towards the somatic aspects of psychological types is the speculation about where Jung himself fell on the somatotype chart. He felt he was an IT type. At least from the publication of Kretschmer's *Physique and Character*, in the same year as *Psychological Types*, the schizophrenic had been identified with the aesthenic, or in Sheldon's terminology, the ectomorphic physique, while Jung had previously associated schizophrenia with regressive introversion. It would be natural, therefore, for him to associate introversion with the ectomorphic physique, and Jung was not at all the typical ectomorph. He had been nick-named by his school friends the barrel, and the Indians at the Taos pueblo had thought that the bear was his appropriate totem. He impressed many of his visitors not only with his height but with his burliness. Jung, himself, was aware of the apparent incongruity between his psychological type and his body type. In writing in 1929 to a woman who was attempting a portrait of him he says, "My exterior is in a strange contrast to my spirit. When I am dead nobody will think that this is the corpse of one with spiritual aspirations. I am the clash of opposites." (Letters, V. 1, p. 51)

The incongruity that Jung felt between his psychological attitude and his body type is a good illustration of the difficulties that have to be overcome in order to correlate the two typologies. Oversimplification of, for example, the IT as always a thin, linear ectomorph will lead to a rejection of the whole relationship.

Common Ground

In considering the evidence for a relationship between Jung's and Sheldon's typologies, it is important to recognize that there is a common ground that is embraced in various ways by Jung, Kretschmer and Sheldon, and the factor analysis school as well. It centers on the basic equation of ectomorphy with introversion, and endomorphy and mesomorphy with extraversion. This insight can be traced to before the time of Jung and Kretschmer and is imbedded in a common sense understanding of body types. The importance of this common ground should not be underestimated. It could serve as the starting point of an increased dialogue among students of individual differences, and it is a giant step towards the goal of establishing a more detailed correlation between somatotype and psychological type. Once we admit the introversion of ectomorphs and the extraversion of endomorphs and mesomorphs, we are already within a context that admits the possibility of finer differentiations and correlations. The next step is admittedly a big one to make, for it is a question of the complete Jungian typology in relation to somatotypes. We have already indicated the struggle Jung underwent to move from a consideration of introversion and extraversion to one of the various kinds of the attitudes. Once these nuances are appreciated, and we have gone from Kretschmer's type descriptions to Sheldon's emphasis on the components of physique and temperament, the way is open to try to go beyond the initial relationship of introversion, extraversion and somatotype.

Psychological Types Implicit in Sheldon's Work

As indicated in chapter 3, we can try to diagnose psychological types in Sheldon's temperament descriptions. We will make use of some of the material in his *Varieties of Delinquent Youth* in the same way later in this chapter. This whole process could be carried out in much greater detail using, for example, the major case studies of *The Varieties of Temperament*. On the whole, this kind of approach is not particularly satisfying because it has to rely on circumstantial evidence and faint clues. There is, however, a convergence of Jung's and Sheldon's descriptions that is best explained by the hypothesis that the two descriptions are describing one complete type at different levels and with different terminology. This convergence is not completely accidental, for Sheldon, as we have seen, was acquainted with Jung. Sheldon's concept of intuition, for example, in *Psychology and the Promethean Will* (1936) appears to be influenced by his contact with Jung which had taken place just prior to the writing of this book. A careful examination, however, of Sheldon's use of the terminology introversion and extraversion, and his citations of Jung, makes it clear that he never went beyond the common ground and never focused on the way the functions differentiate the attitudes in Jung's work. The convergence that is found is based much more on the natural affinities of the typologies for each other than on any desire for Sheldon to explicitly incorporate Jung's psychological types.

Experiments, Formal and Informal

In our initial work on the somatotype-psychological type question, we started with a group of people whose psychological types were clear to us based on observation and interaction over a long period of time. Then we informally somatotyped and determined the temperament of this group by observation. We were not concerned with arriving at an exact numerical rating for either somatotype or temperament, but at least the relative predominance of the components at each level. This period of observation gave rise to a hypothesis which was substantially the same as that which is now presented in Figure 3. With this hypothesis in hand, we then looked for a way in which to test it against already existing data. One important way we found to do this was to make use of the somatotype data that Sheldon and his colleagues had collected, and compare it with the psychological type material that had been generated by the use of the Myers Briggs Type Indicator.

A Somatotype-Psychological Type Experiment

Sheldon provides in the *Atlas of Men* a breakdown of three populations by somatotypes: 4,000 college men, 4,000 college women and 46,000 American males. We can convert these samples to psychological types by applying our somatotype-psychological type hypothesis, and then compare the results to the various MBTI samples.

The samples for 4,000 college men and 4,000 college women are summarized in the form of two somatotype charts in the *Atlas of Men*. After superimposing the somatotype-psychological type hypothesis on the charts, we counted the dots that fell in each area, and then arrived at the percentage figure for each psychological type. Because of the difference in men and women somatotypes, we have used Parnell's method (1958) of shifting the center of gravity of the women's somatotype chart to the southwest, to the 433.

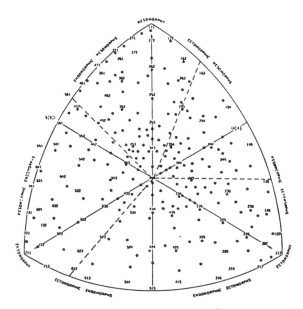

Fig. 6. 4,000 College Men and Psychological Types

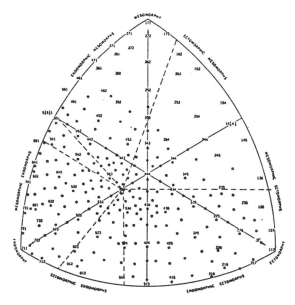

Fig. 7. 4,000 College Women and Psychological Types

For the sample of 46,000 American men which is tabulated by incidence per thousand by somatotypes, we superimposed the somatotype-psychological type hypothesis on Sheldon's somatotype chart (Figure 10, *Varieties of Human Physique*) that shows the area that each somatotype occupied, based on the incidence of the somatotype. On this basis we assigned each somatotype to a psychological type. Where the psychological type line cut through a somatotype area, we assigned half value of that somatotype to each of the adjoining psychological types with the following exceptions: 443 and 442 divided 2/3 ES vs. 1/3 ITS and IFS; 541 and 542 divided 2/3 ES vs. 1/3 ITS and IFS; while the 444 was split into 8 parts.

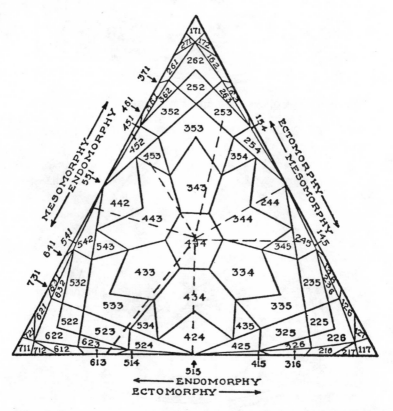

Fig. 8. Somatotype Territory and Psychological Type Territory

130

The MBTI data comes from Myers (1962) and Myers and Myers (1980). We chose the 3,503 high school students, college prep, a common basic sample used in MBTI comparisons, and two other samples to form a rough match with Sheldon's college men and women:

Sample	Introversion	Extraversion
46,000 American males (Sheldon)	38.7	63.0
3,503 high school college prep males (MBTI)	38.5	61.5
4,000 college men (Sheldon)	41.5	57.0
3,676 liberal arts college males (MBTI)	45.7	54.3
4,000 college women (Sheldon)	50.1	50.1
240 Pembroke college women (MBTI)	42.3	58.0

Table 1. Percentage of Introversion and Extraversion by MBTI and Somatotype

The convergence of these results can be viewed as evidence in favor of a somatotype-psychological type correlation. It also could be seen as a confirmation of the reliability of the MBTI extraversion-introversion scores on large samples.

There are a number of points to consider:

1. The samples are only a rough match. It would be better to have a sample for American women from the somatotype direction, and adult men and women from the MBTI, as well as matching samples of the same kinds of college students.

2. Both sets of samples share a trend towards introversion in the college sample.

3. From a theoretical point of view the introversion-extraversion scores of the MBTI probably possess a higher degree of accuracy than the other scores. This is simply because introversion-extraversion is easier to measure. The introversion-extraversion scores by somatotype will also tend to be more accurate because they involve only a few divisions of the whole sample.

4. The problems of whether to somatotype women in the same fashion as men, and where the division lines between the types should fall, make more detailed comparisons difficult. Further, the MBTI scoring of women and men in thinking and feeling could probably be refined.

A further analysis of the 3,503 males from MBTI and Sheldon's 46,000 males by specific type, though premature, is none-the-less interesting. The most prevalent type in each case is the ET-EF type (32.3 MBTI and 27.7 Sheldon). Table 2 shows the eight types compared by percentage of type in the MBTI sample and the Sheldon sample.

Type	Sheldon (46,000 males)	MBTI (3,503 males)
ET-EF	27.8	32.3
ES	20.2	14.2
IU	19.1	6.8
EU	15.1	15.0
IT-IF	14.5	19.7
IS	5.1	12.1

Table 2. Percentage of Type by MBTI and Somatotype

The greatest discrepancy exists between the IS and the IU types. This problem will reappear later when we examine the psychological type of schizophrenics both from the point of view of the MBTI and from somatotypes. One possibility is that the IS territory should be expanded to embrace part of the IU territory and part of the ES territory. This would lower the figures for the ES and IU Sheldon figures and bring them more in line with the MBTI data. The other possibility is that the MBTI figures are weighted in favor of the IS, or finally, a combination of both reasons is at the bottom of these discrepancies.

If we make the assumption that the MBTI results, while being more accurate in determining the predominant components, will be less accurate in determining which function is the primary function and which is the auxiliary, we can group the MBTI results according to the following categories: ETS (EFS) and EST

(ESF); EUT (EUF) and ETU (EFU); IST (ISF) and ITS (IFS); IUT (IUF) and ITU (IFU), thus combining the functions into groups most likely to be mistaken for each other. These groupings can be compared by MBTI and somatotype.

Type	Sheldon (46,000 males)	MBTI (3,503 males)
ETS-EST	36.3	36.3
EUT-ETU	26.8	25.2
IST-ITS	13.0	21.6
IUT-ITU	25.7	16.9

Table 3. Combination of Type MBTI and Somatotype

Again the major discrepency exists in the IS-IU area.

A Temperament-Psychological Type Experiment

There is one study that attempted to determine the correlations between Sheldon's and Jung's typologies by means of objective testing. Ralph Metzner (1980) administered the Cortes-Gatti Self-Description of Temperament Quiz, the Gray-Wheelwright Psychological Type Test and the Eysenck Personality Inventory to a group of 60 men and 96 women who were attending a conference of The Association for Research and Enlightenment at Virginia Beach, Virginia.

He found a positive correlation between mesotonia and extraversion in both men and women, the extraversion being measured by the Eysenck Personality Inventory. He also found a negative correlation between ectotonia and extraversion. These follow the generally found relationships between ectomorphy and introversion, and mesomorphy and extraversion.

More important were the correlations he found that have a bearing on the relationship between the Jungian functions and the

Sheldonian components of temperament. In the male sample, he found a positive correlation between intuition and extraversion, and a negative one between sensation and extraversion. When he compared the functions tested by the Gray-Wheelwright with the three components of temperament, he found in the male sample a positive correlation between intuition and mesotonia, and a negative one between intuition and ectotonia. He also found a negative correlation between sensation and mesotonia, and a positive one between sensation and ectotonia. There are two groupings: extraversion, intuition, mesotonia and a negative correlation to ectotonia forming the first, and introversion, sensation, ectotonia and a negative correlation to mesotonia forming the second. They can be viewed as the two sides of the extraverted intuition type. In the EU type, according to our hypothesis, intuition will appear extraverted, as well as mesotonic, but opposed to the ectotonic, introverted pole. The sensation of the EU type will come out introverted, negatively related to the extraverted pole of mesotonia, but positively related to the introverted pole of ectotonia.

It is not unreasonable to assume that the EU type is being measured at significant levels. The Association for Research and Enlightenment deals with the work of Edgar Cayce, and it would not be surprising to find it attracting a considerable percentage of EU types. Our analysis of Sheldon's correlations between the morphological components and the psychiatric evaluations will show a similar tendency for the EU type to be positively correlated to mesotonia, and negatively correlated to ectotonia.

Indirect Comparisons

While it is true that direct comparisons between somatotype, temperament and psychological type will shed the most light on the relationships between them, indirect comparisons, created by comparing, for example, somatotype and psychological type to a common third thing, would also be interesting and worth doing. Formal indirect comparisons of this kind are difficult to do because of the difference in the samples that are available and in the procedures used to gather them. In the following comparisons we have simply selected some highlights that agree with our overall hypothesis of the relationship between somatotype and psychological type. We have done this in order to encourage, if possible, careful comparisons between these two areas.

1. Myers (1960) compared the MBTI and Strong Vocational Interest Blank scores of 727 male freshmen, while Parnell (1958) examined the somatotype and the choice of faculty of 2,866 male freshmen upon entering Birmingham University (Great Britain). In the case of mathematics the MBTI results indicated a preference for introversion, intuition and thinking, while Parnell found the highest concentration of somatotypes in the endormorphic-ectomorphic range, which is the equivalent to our IU type. In the same way, in the interest of physics, Myers found the same type elements predominated, while Parnell found the highest concentration of somatotypes among the mesomorphic ectomorphs, which we are taking to be equivalent to the IU and IT types.

2. Deabler, Hartl and Willis (1975) somatotyped and gave the SVIB to 300 male subjects. They found, for example, a significant correlation between psychology and ectomorphy. Myers, in the previous cited study, found a strong preference for the intuitive function among psychologists. Under the category of purchasing agent, Myers found the elements of extraversion, sensation and thinking predominating, while the Deabler study found a positive correlation with endomorphy.

3. In a comparison of MBTI scores with the Allport-Vernon-Lindzey Value Scores, Myers (1962) found a correlation between aesthetic interests and introversion and intuition. This fits very well with Sheldon's (1942) correlation of ectotonia and aesthetic intelligence. In the same way, Myers found a correlation between political interests and extraversion, sensation and thinking, while Sheldon in various places indicated the endomorphic mesomorphic build of political figures. The same type preferences, E, S, T, were found by Myers for economic interests, and these, too, fit Sheldon's comments about the endomorphic mesomorphic build of many businessmen.

4. Myers (1962) compared MBTI results with the Personality Research Inventory. She found that *gregariousness* was correlated with E, S, as well as *social know-how*. Both traits are similar to qualities ascribed by Sheldon to the endotonic, which we have related to the ES personality. She also found a relationship between *self-sufficiency* and I,U,T, and between

liking to use the mind and U,T. These findings are in line with Sheldon's traits of the ectotonic and our equation with the IU personality.

5. Myers (1962) compared the MBTI results with faculty ratings of student characteristics. She found traits like *solitary* related to introversion and intuition, and *deep, shows originality, imaginative*, all related to intuition, as well as *good grasp of the abstract* and *independent*. All these ectotonic traits could be applied to the range of psychological types running from the IU through the IT to the EU. The trait *pleasant* was related to extraversion, sensation and feeling, while the traits *cooperative, poor at analyzing* and *willing to take directions* were all correlated to sensation. These are all close to Sheldon's endotonic traits which we have related to the ES personality.

6. Myers (1962) found that the IU type had the highest mean I.Q.s and the highest mean grade point averages. This matches Sheldon's (1942) correlation of ectotonia and I.Q. Parnell (1958) also found a relationship between academic performance and ectomorphy, which also fits in with our correlation between ectomorphy-ectotonia-IU. Both Sheldon and Parnell found that the 225 somatotype was the somatotype that most distinguished itself academically, and the 225 falls right in the middle of the territory we have delineated as that of the IU type.

Following the 225 somatotype in academic performance was the 523. If we look at the somatotype chart, this falls right near the IS, ES boundary. Myers found that the IST, along with the EUT, have the highest grade point averages after the IU types. Myers felt that the superior performance of the IU type could not be attributed to their higher I.Q. or application, and felt it could be a habit of mind which produces a certain interest in academic kinds of activities. Sheldon, looking at the same issue from the perspective of somatotypes, felt that somatotypes like the 225 and the 523 did not have the distraction from academic pursuits because of their low mesomorphy that divided the time and energy of many other types. Both of these considerations seem roughly equivalent, and could form the starting point of a consideration of I.Q. differences among groups in virtue of the relative frequency of the different types within the groups.

7. Myers (1962) reported on a four-year study of employee turn-over by Laney where the turn-over rate of intuitive workers

was much higher than that of sensing workers, especially in mechanical jobs. This can be compared with Parnell's report of a study of Bullen where among female factory workers who were engaged in piece-work stitching, the mesomorphic-endomorphic women lasted the longest. Linear women had a higher turn-over rate. These results are also consistent with our conversions of somatotype to psychological type.

These are not the only areas where comparisons might be fruitful. Sheldon describes a number of three-way traits which distinguish the three components of temperament. For example, in reaction to trouble, the endotonic needs and seeks out people, the mesotonic needs action, and the ectotonic solitude. Or in the case of alcohol, the endotonic becomes more relaxed and sociophilic, the mesotonic becomes more aggressive and assertive, and the ectotonic becomes more resistant to alcohol and depressed by it. Attitude towards death and privacy preferences can also be viewed as three-way temperamental traits. All of these traits could serve as common points of comparison for somatotype, temperament and psychological type evaluations.

Sheldon also made observations about the somatotype and temperament type of delinquent boys, temperamental susceptibility to hypnosis, and to heat and cold sensitivity, sleeping styles, space and housing preferences, and many other things. These could be compared to psychological type evaluation of the same traits. These kinds of comparisons will serve not only as further evidence for a correlation between the three levels of type, but also serve to clarify and delineate the interrelationships between these levels and help knit them together into one typological instrument with many possible applications.

Continuity and Discontinuity

Sheldon's somatotypes are described as an ever-varying continuum while Jung's psychological types are distinct entities set off rather sharply from each other. These two modes of descriptions seem on the surface to be strongly opposed to each other and an obstacle to the integration of somatotypes, temperament and psychological types.

If discontinuity can be demonstrated underlying Sheldon's somatotypes, the problem will begin to resolve itself and incidentally serve as another kind of evidence in favor of the relationship between the two typologies. The young men who were the subjects of Sheldon's *Varieties of Delinquent Youth* were strongly clustered in the endomorphic-mesomorphic northwest of the somatotype chart. If we study the capsule biographies of the majority of the men who were somatotyped 451 and 452, two distinct patterns emerge.

The first is a series of cases where mesomorphy has been rated at 5 and endomorphy at 4 or 4½. The descriptions seem more appropriate for the ES than for the ET. For example, case 18, a 4 ½ 5 1½, evokes the comments, "Although powerfully built, he can neither fight nor run, but he swims fairly well. He is emotionally extraverted, relaxed, gluttonous, also stubborn and surly. The youth has held a job for nearly a year, is fatter, seems more dull and bleary." Case 192, a 451½, is described as: "sociable, happiest where the crowd is thickest and noisiest, enormous energy combined with a total absence of physical combativeness."

In the other series mesomorphy advances to a 5½, while endomorphy remains at 4. These young men are described in quite a different way. Case 164, a 45½ 1½, is seen as: "of tremendous energy, he seems to have a constant need for letting off steam in dangerous actions, his unlimited courage, directness, psychological callousness, and lack of restraint define extreme somatotonia (mesotonia.)" And case 200, a 45½2, "a picture of relaxed, resourceful and aggressive somatotonia (mesotonia) without a smile. Behind the menace lies both physical power and a violent, destructive temper. He looks upon life through the eyes of a predator." Table 4 gives the somatotypes of these two series, and Figure 9 shows them represented on the somatotype chart.

EST			ETS		
Case	VDY	VDY 30	Case	VDY	VDY 30
12	4½51½	451½	13	45½1½	45½1½
18	4½51½	55½1	90	45½1½	35½1½
23	452	64½2	118	45½1½	451
47	4½52	4½53	164	45½1½	45½2
120	4½52½	55½2½	193	45½1½	35½1½
172	4½52	44½3½	195	45½1	3½5½1½
192	451½	452½	200	45½2	2½62½

Table 4. Selected EST and ETS cases in VDY and VDY 30

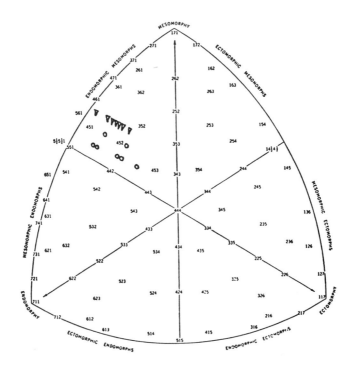

Fig. 9. VDY Cases

If we avert simply to somatotype we would conclude that the underlying temperaments and psychological type would be quite close. The half point in mesomorphy should not have such an impact as to strongly differentiate the people involved, yet a reading of the cases indicated that there are two distinct types involved. With the publication of *Physique and Delinquent Behavior, A Thirty-Year Follow-Up of William H. Sheldon's*

Varieties of Delinquent Youth by Emil M. Hartl, Edward P. Monnelly and Roland D. Elderkin (1982) we were able to pursue this question further. The young men were re-somatotyped by using Sheldon's Trunk Index method. If our original assumption was correct, the re-somatotyping to the degree it corrected the original somatotypes should show the cases we labeled ES moving towards the endomorphic pole, while the cases we labelled ET should move towards the mesomorphic pole.

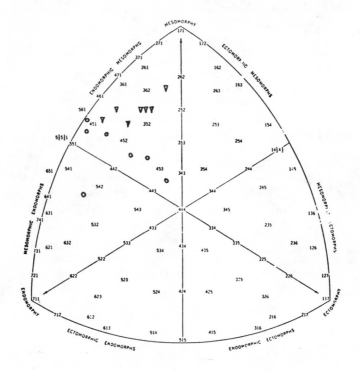

Fig. 10. VDY 30 Cases

This kind of discontinuity which can also be seen in the Gabriel and Eugene cases in the *Varieties of Temperament* cannot be explained adequately within the framework of somatotype alone. If we imagine a psychological type boundary running through the 451-452 area, then the divergence of the types on either side becomes comprehensible.

While there is a certain amount of evidence supporting the hypothesis of a relationship between somatotypes, temperament and psychological types, with the availability of proper personnel and facilities, a much more rigorous and conclusive kind of testing could be carried out. This would be best done by a number of independent teams. The first would somatotype the subjects, while the second consisting of two or three independent observers would attempt to establish the temperament type by observation, interview and written testing. The third team, again composed of two or three diagnosticians, would evaluate the psychological type in the same way. The subject whose temperament and psychological types are agreed upon by the observers in each team would then be the final subjects for a comparison of somatotype, temperament and psychological type. This kind of experimentation would go beyond what is possible by the use of written testing alone and would go a long way in determining the precise relationship between these three levels of type.

Chapter 9

The Implications of
an Integrated Typology

There are many consequences if the relationship we have presented is true. We have already discussed the heightened objectivity and visibility it gives to psychological types and its corollary in the greater ease in which typological identification can be made.

It also leads to the possibility of the quantification of psychological type in the same numerical fashion as Sheldon's somatotype, temperament index and psychiatric index. More importantly, we are confronted with the question of whether there is genuine variability of the psychological type within its own territory. Is the 632 ES, for example, really the same as the 451 ES? And does this variation have something to do with the actual structuring of the functions with one another? Are people different, not only in attitude and function, but also in the internal configuration of the functions in terms of the distance of one function from another, that is, in terms of psychological accessibility? Is integration harder for some people than for others because of this kind of articulation? When seen in this light, Sheldon's remarks on the 444 temperament are potentially significant. These people exhibit a greater ability to develop in different directions, but do they also exhibit a higher degree of susceptibility to neurosis, i.e., the unwanted intrusion of unconscious material into consciousness? In the same way, does the extreme polar physique have more difficulty in integrating the auxiliary functions? Are some people naturally closer to their inferior function? Such questions, if they become answerable, could have an important effect on actual therapeutic practice and provide a way to differentiate what kinds of techniques to use in different cases.

The integration of Sheldon's constitutional psychology with Jung's psychological types, and thus with his whole psychology, allows for the development of the therapeutic possibilities of Sheldon's works. These he did not energetically pursue because he felt that the prior work of description must be carried out first. Beyond the fundamental aspects of somatotype and temperament, there are important secondary concepts in Sheldon's work like dysplasia and the andric-gynic index which can also provide valuable tools for a person's self-understanding. Dysplasia, for example, can be objectively portrayed by the use of the Structural Profile, and yield a graphic representation of how the individual differs from the norms of the group that he lives in. A thorough discussion of Sheldon's principle to never reverse a person's morphological predominances would complement any discussion of the psychological functions and how their development is effected by the environment. Sheldon was aware that his constitutional analysis could be carried out conjointly with psychoanalysis, with one starting from flesh and bone and extending as far up as it could go, while the other started from consciousness and went as far down as it could go.

The quantification of psychological types, while somewhat problematical, might have a valuable payoff in terms of trying to analyze the difference between natural type and environmental type at all three levels, and the connection that these differences have in terms of personal growth and maladjustment. Sheldon tried to do this on the level of body and temperament type in the *Varieties of Temperament.* How far can someone diverge from their natural typological dispositions and still be in good health? If phenotype and genotype in this limited sense could be distinguished and measured quantitatively on all three levels, then there would be the possibility of answering these kinds of questions.

Typology, Biochemistry and Genetics

The relationship between somatotypes and psychological types opens up the possibility of exploring in a systematic fashion the biochemical and genetic foundations of typology. Somatotype is the first step in the formulation of what could be called biochemical type or chemotype (Cortes and Gatti, 1972). What

Sheldon did on the anatomical plane he felt could be extended into the area of endocrinology and even as far as the cell itself. The nature and extent of man's biochemical individuality is an important correction to the tendency to talk about norms in blood pressure, basal metabolism, brain and muscle structure and size, etc. (Williams, 1956). But we cannot choose between individual diversity on the one hand and universal statements on the other. Both have their place, and in the middle, as a sort of mediating bridge, is the idea of typology, but now in terms of biochemical type.

Who are the people who have the largest hearts and circulatory systems per body weight, or the largest digestive systems, or the most developed nervous systems? Are there ways to group the variations of metabolism instead of saying above normal or below normal? In short, how far can body types act as the centers of organization around which this kind of information can form meaningful groups of distinctive biochemical traits? Can a biochemical portrait be drawn for each somatotype, and thus each psychological type? Then the full range of type would extend from the basic structure and organization of the psyche down to the particular kind of biochemical type. This kind of work is in its infancy, but it promises to be fruitful for the medical doctor and the psychotherapist, both of whom must treat the whole man.

It is but another aspect of the same question to ask about the genetic foundation of type. No one would be surprised at there being a genetic basis to somatotype, for we associate the body and genetics, but the unravelling of the genetics of temperament, psychological type and psychopathology is just beginning.

Typology taken in the wide sense of an integrated typology can play an important role as a basic descriptive framework that could allow the integration and translation of data from biochemical, genetic and psychological studies. It can provide a conceptual structure that is flexible enough to coordinate information from the different sciences that contribute to an understanding of human differences. It may be helpful to take some practical examples to illustrate the possible use of typology in this way, without presuming to make any statements about the disciplines themselves.

Type and Coronary Heart Disease

A cardiologist can look at his work from several different points of view. He could draw a portrait of the probable genetic factors that predispose a person to coronary heart disease, or one of the possible biochemical mechanisms that brings about the actual disease. He could also draw up a list of physical factors that increase the risk of the disease, and a psychological portrait of the traits in the coronary-prone personality, with a number of factors that influence these traits. Once he had looked at the subject from all these different points of view, he could attempt to integrate this knowledge. What we are suggesting is that a typology such as can be developed from Jung's and Sheldon's work could serve as a framework, not only to integrate these particular viewpoints, but to be used as a common language that would describe not only the coronary-prone personality, but people subject to other major

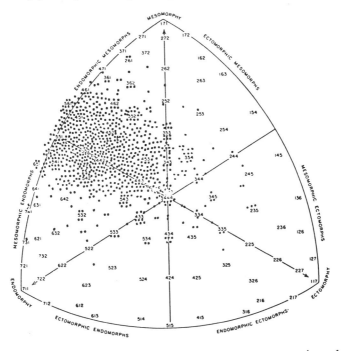

Fig. 11. Coronary Heart Disease Somatotypes. Dupertuis and Dupertuis

disorders like diabetes, cancer, peptic ulcer, etc. The language of typology is implicit in many of the descriptions that the cardiologist gives. For example, in the area of somatotype, cardiologists have observed that the cardiac patient appears neither excessively obese nor tall and lean, at least in the younger age brackets. Sheldon made similar observations.

In extensive studies of the somatotypes of heart disease patients, Dupertuis and Dupertuis found that they were strongly massed in the endomorphic-mesomorph and mesomorphic-endomorph territories. Figure 11 shows the somatotype distribution of 837 male whites with arteriosclerotic heart disease. These somatotype territories we have assigned to the ETS (EFS), EST (ESF), and possibly the ITS (IFS).

Somatotype allows the possibility of refining the clinical information about the coronary-prone personality by making the normal guidelines more selective and relevant. It could theoretically answer, for example, the question of what is the normal blood pressure for those people from whom a large percentage of the coronary victims are drawn, or the normal cholesterol levels, etc.

Even though the somatotypes of the coronary patients are tightly grouped, it is possible to distinguish between the somatotype of short and long term survivors among cardiac patients (Dupertuis and Dupertuis, 1968). The short-term survivors tend to be more mesomorphic, while the long-term survivors tend to be more balanced in endomorphy and mesomorphy, or more endomorphic.

There are also temperament and psychological type descriptions implicit in the portrait of the coronary-prone personality. We shall simply list some of the characteristics drawn from the work of Friedman and Rosenman, 1974, and C. David Jenkins, 1975. They include: competitiveness, aggressiveness, love of action, explosive accentuation of speech and laughter, excessive energy for action, rapid eating, guilt about relaxation, limited introversion, leadership in a competitive situation, and a total commitment to the job at hand. These characteristics read like Sheldon's check-list of mesotonia, and each one of them can be duplicated from Sheldon's description of the mesotonic found in the *Varieties of Temperament*. Furthermore, it is possible to view many of the other traits of the coronary-prone personality as exaggerations of this basic personality structure, for example, the chronic sense of time urgency, haste, impatience, hyperalertness, the doing of multiple jobs simultaneously, the inability to relate to things or people not job-related. All these qualities fit the picture of the one-sided mesotonic extraverted thinking personality.

In the study of somatotype and survivorship previously cited, the short-term survivors were described as being "more apprehensive about their illness, more reluctant to accept any limitations in their physical expression or their role as head of the household and breadwinner, and more opposed to any show of sympathy or protectiveness by other members of the family. It appeared also that the short-term survivors as a group exhibited a persona that was more out-going, aggressive, energetic and restless than was true for the long-term survivors. The latter group seemed more able to accept their 'fate' and appeared to be more relaxed and willing to adapt to the situation in which they found themselves." (1968, p. 96).

The parallelism between the somatotype based description and that of the coronary prone personality which, as far as we know, developed independently of each other, is too striking to be ignored. It illustrates the possibility of using typological language as a basic framework within which to place biochemical, genetic, social factors, etc. It also suggests the possibility of using Jung's model of the individuation process to find ways to modify the behavior of Type A personalities. The differentiation between long and short term survivors in what first appears to be a rather homogenous group of cardiac patients is strikingly similar to the differentiation we have noted in the Delinquent Youth series, and could be interpreted in the same fashion, i.e., that underlying the somatotype distribution are two distinct psychological type territories.

Type and Psychopathology

A psychiatrist specializing in schizophrenia, for example, could, like his colleague the cardiologist, draw a number of portraits of the schizophrenic. He could do this in terms of the genetic predisposition, or the possible biochemical mechanisms, or the physical factors that might precipitate the outbreak of the disease, or he could make a psychological portrait of the schizophrenic personality and the social factors that have influenced it. Then he could attempt to integrate this wide range of knowledge. Here, again, typology, taken in the broader sense, could serve as a useful organizational framework. Since both Jung and Sheldon devoted a great deal of time and energy to the study of schizophrenia, as well as to the other psychiatric illnesses, it will be useful to list very briefly some contributions to the field of typology in psychiatry so we can look at the problem from a slightly better historical perspective. An extensive summary from the point of view of somatotype can be found in Rees (1961).

Jung, in his 1913 paper that announced his interest in types, identifies the schizophrenic as an introvert, albeit a regressed introvert, and the hysteric as a regressed extravert. Kretschmer, in 1921 in *Physique and Character*, described the aesthenic physique of the schizophrenic, and the pyknic physique of the manic-depressive. The common ground we saw between body type and normal personality extends into psychopathology in the form of the observation that schizophrenics tend to be ectomorphic and introverted (leptosomatic) while manic-depressives tend to be endomorphic-mesomorphic (pyknics), and extraverted. Implicit, also, in Jung's and Sheldon's and Kretschmer's work is a view of psychiatric illness which comprises not only a dimension of personality, but that of a biochemical disorder as well. This type of thinking has been made explicit by Eysenck who envisioned two orthogonal axes: one of introversion and extraversion, and the other of psychoticism. Gray and Wheelwright (1946) summarized some of the early studies that confirmed the relationship between introversion and schizophrenia, and extraversion and manic-depressive disease.

Van Der Hoop in 1937, drawing on both Jung and Kretschmer, tentatively identified the schizophrenic with the IU and the IS type, and the manic-depressive with the ES and the EU type. K.W. Bash (1961), while not relating the specific psychological type to the various kinds of psychopathology, does examine the psychological function in relationship to psychiatric illnesses. Delusion and illusion, for example, are related to the function of intuition. Bisbee, Mullaly and Osmond (1982) gave the MBTI to 372 psychiatric patients close to their time of admission, and found that schizophrenic patients tended to be more introverted with the IST and the ISF and the IFS predominating, while the manic-depressives were more extraverted with the EFS, EUT, and IFU types over-represented.

Sheldon, while visiting Kretschmer's clinic, conceived the possibility of reformulating Kretschmer's type descriptions in terms of basic components and quantifying them. What he was aiming at was a biologically-founded psychiatric language that would go beyond the traditional Kraepelinian terminology and link up with normal psychology in terms of the descriptive framework of somatotype and temperament. He did extensive work in this direction (1949, 1969), which is still well worth reading. This work led him to hypothesize that manic-depressive psychosis, paranoid schizophrenia and hebephrenic schizophrenia could all be described as the absence of one of the major components of somatotype and temperament. He felt that the hebephrenic schizophrenic lacked mesomorphy, the paranoid schizophrenic lacked endomorphy, and the manic-depressive lacked ectomorphy. Therefore, the psychiatric poles on the somatotype chart would fall opposite the somatotype and temperament poles. Sheldon had started on the difficult road of reformulating psychiatric types into a broader framework of normal psychology and basic components that could be quantified when he had come in contact with Nolan D. C. Lewis' observations on the hypoplastic vascular system of hebephrenic schizophrenics. He went on to enlarge this insight to cover the whole mesodermal endowment: bone, muscle, and connective tissue. The hebephrenic schizophrenic was then characterized as being mesopenic. Arieti (1974) sums up a variety of studies on the cardiovascular apparatus of the schizophrenic that can be interpreted in this light. They include volume of circulating blood, blood pressure, heart size and vasomotor disturbances leading to cyanosis.

If we examine the somatotype charts on which Sheldon (1949) plotted the somatotypes of the hebephrenic schizophrenics, the paranoid schizophrenics and the manic-depressives from his Elgin Hospital study, and superimpose on them the somatotype-psychological type hypothesis, we see that the cluster of manic-depressive patients (Fig. 12) is much like Sheldon anticipated, for they are well-grouped in opposition to the pole of ectomorphy. They fall on the extraverted side of the chart, and it seems that extraverted sensation, but with considerable degrees of mesomorphy, is the predominant type. This agrees fairly well with part of Van Der Hoop's evaluation that the manic-depressive is an ES, but not with his impression that they are EUs. It is also close

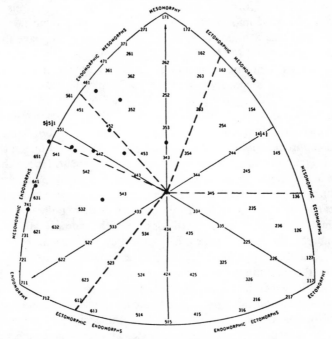

Fig. 12 Manic-Depressive Somatotypes

to the EFS type that Bisbee, Mullaly and Osmond found, but not to their EUT and IFU. Interestingly, both Van Der Hoop and Bisbee et al. point to the EU type. Further, if we read Kretschmer's portrait of Mr. Quick, *a cheery hypomanic personality*, while we are struck by the fact that typologically he appears most like an EST, he also has qualities that are suggestive of the EU personality. It may well be that the EST in a manic-phase of behavior simulates well the quick changeability and innovative character of the EU. Jung was once questioned about the variability of the superior function and stated, "If you consider the case of manic depressive insanity, you occasionally find that in the manic phase one function prevails, and in the depressive phase another function prevails." (V. 18, p. 31). Now that bi-polar depressive disease is being distinguished from uni-polar depressive disease, it would be interesting to see if they could be distinguished on the basis of somatotype as well.

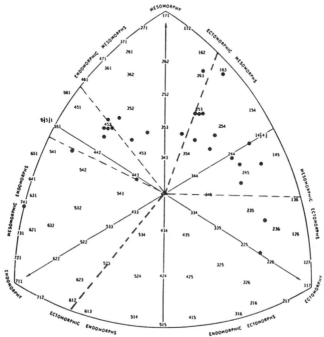

Fig. 13. Paranoid Schizophrenic Somatotypes

In Figure 13 the majority of patients cluster in the area opposite the pole of endomorphy, but there is a leakage to the area of the northwest. Sheldon found that while the manic-depressive component showed a positive correlation with endomorphy (.54) and with mesomorphy (.41) and a negative correlation with ectomorphy (-.59) as he anticipated, the other two psychiatric components did not show the expected correlations. The paranoid component showed a positive correlation with mesomorphy as expected (.57), but instead of a negative correlation with endomorphy, it showed a correlation of .14, and instead of a positive correlation with ectomorphy, it showed a negative correlation (-.34). These unexpected correlations become more comprehensible if we consider that many of the paranoids appear to be EUs, and therefore would not positively correlate with the introverted ectomorphic pole. At the same time, though EUs are in some opposition to the pole of endomorphy (intuition

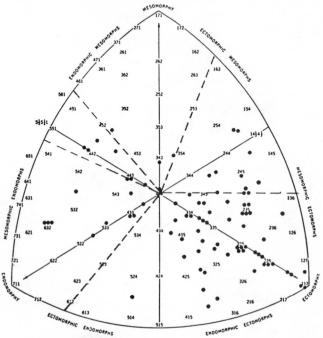

Fig. 14. Hebephrenic Schizophrenic Somatotypes

vs. sensation), the opposition is muted by their common extraversion. The cluster to the northwest we will examine in relationship to Figure 14.

In this chart the cluster of patients, instead of being massed opposite the pole of mesomorphy, is grouped in the southwest corner. Sheldon found that the 3rd psychiatric component showed the expected correlation with ectomorphy (.64) and the expected negative correlation with mesomorphy (-.68), but instead of a positive correlation with endomorphy, there was a negative one of (-.25). Why does the massing take place to the southeast? The answer that suggests itself from the point of view of psychological types is that the IU type is more prevalent than the IS type. This may be due to the particular sample that Sheldon was working with, and he suggests that the patients most lacking in mesomorphy might already have been eliminated, or it may be due as well to the greater predisposition of the IU type to develop schizophrenia. Bisbee, et al. found a high number of IS types among the schizophrenic patients. This may be due to the fact that these patients were actually IS types which had already disappeared from Sheldon's sample, but here, were caught at the beginning of their hospital stay, or it may be due to the fact that the regressive introversion of the schizophrenic IUs makes them appear to be sensation types due to the eruption of the material coming through the inferior function. Parnell's schizophrenic samples (1958) seem to have higher percentages of ISs than Sheldon's.

The leakage towards the 442, 452 area found in the paranoid is even more striking in the case of the hebephrenic schizophrenic because of the absence of subjects in the southeast. One possible explanation for this scattering is that in both cases we are looking at the ITS/IFS population. It may well be that these people are classified either as schizophrenics or paranoids.

The impression of the relationship between the IU personality and the schizophrenic is strengthened when we read the literature that has grown up from Kretschmer to Kety about the schizoid personality. It would be possible to compile a list of traits that would parallel Sheldon's ectotonic check list, as well as the description of the IU personality. This list would include *self-conscious, critical, rigid, meticulous, obstinate, withdrawn, passive, shy, unsociable, seeks solitude, tired, serious*, etc. (Heston, 1973). If a relationship can be established between the schizophrenic and the IU personality, or the manic-depressive and the ES personality, then the way is open to clarify why this person is predisposed to psychopathology, both psychologically and physically. as well as to what state of normalcy he should be expected to return to.

Psychiatric illness, seen within a typological framework, far from being antagonistic to the recent developments in the genetic and biochemical nature of mental illness, is particularly apt to serve as an integrative and unifying framework for this kind of information. If we conceive of typology and psychosis not forming a continuum, but two orthogonal axes, then it is easier to imagine the relationship between the IU and IS type and schizophrenia. There does not have to be any essential relationship between the two. It is possible that the metabolic dysfunctions that appear linked with schizophrenia would express themselves in various ways according to the type of the person involved. Rosenthal et al., in an evaluation of the children of schizophrenics reared in adoptive homes, found data that suggests: "that the inherited core diathesis is the same for both schizophrenia and manic-depressive psychosis, but that manic-depressives may have other modifying genes or life experiences which direct the clinical manifestations of the diathesis in a different way." (1968, p. 387). Thus, the dysfunctions may accentuate the already natural introversion and sensitivity of the IU and IS type, whereas other types may be more resistant to them or express them in a distinct fashion. The paranoid schizophrenics, for example, if their disorder is actually the same kind as the hebephrenic schizophrenic, has a different typology and shows a different course of disease and prognosis. (Kline and Tenney, 1950). The value of the type hypothesis in its integrated form consists in the possibility that if the question of type could be clarified, then it could be extracted from the complex manifestation of the psychopathology. This holds true both for an understanding of the biochemistry involved, as well as the genetics. If the actual disease process is seen as the intersection and interaction of two independent variables, the more refined the typological one becomes, the more the overall understanding of the disease will increase.

Sheldon was well aware of the need to extend his findings about somatotype and mental illness in the direction of biochemistry. At the time he wrote and championed a biological view of mental illness when such a view was not popular, the necessary knowledge was not available for such an integration to take place. What struck Sheldon as forcefully as the relationship of somatotype to schizophrenia was the relationship of a factor of what he called aesthenia. He meant by this the failure of the organism to reach full development, which failure could be detected at the level of the body as a whole, but would have to be pursued at the cellular level. He stated in 1949:

"Whatever the aesthenic estate is at bottom and the burgeoned estate, these are without doubt, expressions of the personality of the cells of the individual...Better understanding of this field is in the future, but it may not be far in the future..." (1949, p. 792).

The diagnostic problem returns with a vengeance when it is a case of personalities with a serious psychiatric illness. Jung made it clear that the schizophrenic who shows an introverted character during the incubation of his illness can reach a stage of morbid compensation where "he seems constrained to draw attention to himself by his extravagant, insupportable, or directly aggressive behavior." (1913). He could then easily be typed at variance to his natural disposition.

The difficulty of typological diagnosis makes it hard to assess studies on the pre-morbid characteristics of schizophrenic children. Type is often difficult to discern in the fluid and unformed personalities of the children, and this problem is compounded by the possibility that the sub-clinical onset of schizophrenia may express itself, as Jung stated, in an acting out coming from the other side of the personality. Thus, shy, withdrawn children might be found rarely to become schizophrenic, while unsocialized aggression could be a prominant characteristic without either finding necessarily contradicting the association or affinity for schizophrenia to express itself in the introverted personalities. Hopefully, the objectivity lent to psychological types by somatotypes will help resolve this problem.

Typology could also play a valuable role in helping unravel the genetics of mental illness. If there is a relationship between psychological type and mental illness, then the genetic base to psychological types, if it could be elucidated, would clarify the role that heredity plays in psychiatric illnesses as well. Psychological types should not remain simply within their traditional boundaries in the context of Jungian analysis or even in its fairly new role as a tool in vocational and educational counseling, etc., but via its integration with body and temperament types, draw more closely to the biochemistry of personality and behavioral genetics.

A Genetic Basis to Psychological Types?

In this section, we would like to discuss briefly some ideas about the genetic mechanisms underlying psychological types. This area is virtually unexplored and we make no pretense to be able to say anything definitive about it. All we would like to do is raise the question in a concrete way that psychological types should be considered from a genetic point of view.

While there is a certain amount of information about the genetic basis to somatotype and temperament, and introversion and extraversion, there is very little that deals directly with the genetics of the whole psychological type or the mechanism involved. Some of the findings for somatotype have been summarized by Rees (1968), and for temperament by Buss and Plomin (1975) and Thomas and Chess (1977), and for psychiatric illness by Sperber and Jarvik (1976). Sheldon, in his 1969 article *Psychotic Patterns*, with Nathan Kline and Ashton Tenney, mentioned a number of studies he made where the somatotype remained constant, or more precisely, the ratio between the chest area and the abdominal area remained the same under varying environmental conditions. These studies included children from the Berkeley Growth Study who had been followed from childhood to adulthood, people from the University of Minnesota starvation experiment, West Pointers upon entering and leaving the Academy after closely supervised body-conditioning programs, and Columbia University students who had been photographed as freshmen and then somatotyped 40 years later. These findings could also be construed to support a genetic view of somatotype. Cortes and Gatti in their study of delinquency devote an appendix to the mostly favorable evidence for a correlation between the 3 components of physique with the 3 layers of the embryo. This also could be understood as support for a genetic basis to Sheldon's somatotypes.

Jung had been impressed by the striking differences to be seen in children with essentially the same home environment. This pointed, he felt, to the inborn nature of psychological types. Eysenck (1956) in a study of identical and fraternal twins, found that the identical twins resembled each other more closely than did the fraternal twins in extraversion-introversion. He summarized the evidence for the heritability of personality in *The*

Biological Basis of Personality (1967). Scarr (1969), studying the results of 10 twin studies, including Eysenck's and her own, found moderate to high genetic contributions to social introversion-extraversion. Horn, Plomin, and Rosenman (1976), while looking for factors that might point to a disposition to develop coronary disease, found a number of traits in which identical twins were more concordant than fraternal twins. One of the most striking was talking to strangers, which is a good indicator of introversion-extraversion.

If there is a relationship between somatotype, temperament and psychological type, and the first two are genetically based, we would expect psychological type to be genetically based as well, and this seems to be borne out as far as introversion and extraversion by the studies we have cited. If, then, we can accept the genetic basis for introversion and extraversion as a fairly well-established fact, the next question concerns the actual genetic mechanism involved. If we accept somatotype as a polygenic characteristic, then we would expect psychological type to be polygenic as well. But this does not mean that it must be simply polygenic. It could include a substantial factor that is X-linked. (McKusick, 1964, p. 22).

Our own impressions gathered from informal family studies are that, while there is no easily observable pattern to the psychological types as a whole, there appears to be a pattern to the introversion and the extraversion in many families. Put in the simplest form, the attitudinal type of the father is often followed by the daughters, while the attitudinal type of the mother is followed by the sons. While this would mean that introverted parents tend to have introverted children, and extraverted parents have extraverted children, to observe this is not particularly striking or unusual. What is more interesting are cases where attitudinal types of the parents differ, and the children are found to be grouped in attitude according to sex.

The hypothesis we would like to propose is that, while psychological type as a whole, i.e., attitude and function, is polygenic, introversion and extraversion could be X-linked. The evidence, while somewhat circumstantial, converges from different directions.

Gary and Glover (1976), extending the work of Morgan Worthy, directed a survey where the answers to a series of simple questions were correlated to dark and light eye color. These questions, for example, about enjoying the company of other people or enjoying parties, could be looked upon as good practical indications of introversion and extraversion. The results indicated a relationship between the dark eyes and extraversion and the light eyes and introversion. This does not mean that there has to be any essential link between eye color and attitude, though this aspect should not be ignored. It does seem to point to the association of eye color and attitude in genetic transmission. Lenski (1977) extended these observations to the question of the relationship between somatotype, race and national differences.

Winge (1921) found a tendency for the eye color of the child to take after that of the parent of the opposite sex. Brues (1946) found some evidence for the occurence of dominant or partially dominant eye color genes on the X-chromosome. We can speculate that both introversion and extraversion, or put in another way, the biochemical mechanism underlying introversion and extraversion and eye color, could be X-linked dominant characteristics. This would explain the patterns that Gary and Glover found.

Another piece of this puzzle can be found in the mounting evidence connecting manic-depressive (bi-polar) disease with X-linked dominant transmission. (Cadoret and Winokur, 1976; Winokur and Tanna, 1969). Sheldon described manic depressives as failing in the mechanisms of inhibition. They lack ectomorphy-ectotonia, or put in another way, they could be called deficient in introversion. It is highly suggestive, then, that a disease that appears like a failure of the introversion-extraversion mechanism should be associated with X-linked dominant transmission.

If introversion and extraversion are X-linked dominant characteristics, then we would expect the somatotypes of the mother and son, or father and daughter, to agree to the extent that both would fall within the territories we have delineated for introversion and extraversion on the somatotype chart. If we look at the major cases that Sheldon described in the *Varieties of Temperament*, and determine the psychological attitude of the men and their mothers simply on the basis of somatotype, they agree in all 6 cases. A further comparison of the siblings of the subjects also shows agreement between child and the parent of the opposite sex with one exception. However, in most cases it appears that the parents share the same attitudinal type, so that the agreement of the children with this attitude is not particularly striking.

Parnell (1958) in a study of 45 families, found a strong tendency for the child's somatotype to fall on or near a line drawn between the somatotypes of the parents when plotted on the basic somatotype chart. If we take this line principle as an expression of the polygenic nature of somatotypes, then we would expect it would also, in some fashion, express the X-linked nature of introversion and extraversion within this polygenic framework. If we examine the 45 cases and tentatively determine the introversion and extraversion of the child in relationship to that of the parent of the opposite sex by plotting the somatotypes on our chart that shows both somatotypes and psychological type, we find that out of the 45, 42 are in fairly close agreement and can be interpreted in terms of the child and the parent of the opposite sex sharing either introversion or extraversion. The cases that show a notable departure are cases 11, 19 and 20. Parnell found a number of cases that departed from his line principle. One of the cases that he pointed out as departing from it was case 11. Cases 19 and 20 also depart from the line principle. From the point of view of somatotype, Parnell's work can be seen as converging towards the results that come from other areas.

Parnell (1959) reported on another study where men entering Birmingham University (Great Britain) were somatotyped, and then chose the somatotype of their fathers and mothers from a series of photographs. He then plotted the somatotypes of the parents for the men who had chosen their own somatotype correctly. The results are in fairly close agreement to our expectations that the somatotypes of the sons will fall in the introverted territories if the somatotype of the mother falls in the introverted territories, and vice versa for extraversion. For example, in a distribution of sons who chose 462 as the father's somatotype, and 2 1/2 2 6 as the mother's, 8 out of 11 fell in introverted territories. In a distribution of sons who estimated their father as 344 and their mother as 334, 9 out of 12 fell within the introverted territories.

There are limitations to these kinds of comparisons. First there are obvious limitations springing from how the somatotypes of the parents were determined. Secondly, both father and mother were somatotyped, as is reasonable, on the same chart, but there is a strong possibility that the relationship between somatotype and psychological type is distributed differently in each case. Brues (1950), however, in an article entitled *Linkage of Body Build with Sex, Eye Color and Freckling* concluded that X-linked factors may be involved in the genetic foundation of body build.

Worthy, concluding his study of eye color and behavior, indicates the evidence for the X-linked nature of the genetic mechanism that might be involved. This evidence includes sex differences in reactivity between men and women in which women appear more reactive than men, and the X-linked nature of certain spatial visualization abilities (Stafford, 1961) (Garron, 1970). It may be possible to link these factors to somatotype-psychological type. The distribution of women's somatotypes, for example, is massed closer to the endomorphic pole than men's, and thus to the extraverted side as well. It remains an open question whether spatial visualization can be connected with introversion and intuition.

We are left with the overall impression that the X-linked nature of introversion and extraversion is a hypothesis well worth pursuing. What is needed are careful family studies of introversion and extraversion, or more exactly, complete typological analyses of whole families which will include somatotype, temperament, and psychological type. While somatotyping provides no real difficulties, psychological typing is, as we have seen, more complex. It is possible to see that if introversion and extraversion are tested for outside the context of the whole psychological type, the results can often be difficult to decipher. If we draw a portrait of the introverted thinker, and try to compare him with the introverted sensation type on the basis of introversion alone, this comparison can be difficult if we are not familiar with the different kinds of introversion that exist. Further, the best way to gather family psychological type data is by a slow process of interview and observation in which tests can help, but not substitute for the whole procedure.

Further Type Applications

Typology can integrate, within the framework it erects, all kinds of particular knowledge. The portraits of individual types could eventually be extended to color preferences, graphology, conceptions of space and time (Mann, Siegler, Osmond, 1968), and possibly even to the lateralization of the brain (Rossi, 1977). Typology as a science of human differences has an enormous potential range of application. It can provide exploratory hypotheses, which are vital tools of understanding, by which we attempt to grasp more and more particular facts under wider and wider headings, and thus make the facts usable.

Jung's typology is already being applied to learning styles and preferences (Silver & Hanson) (Keirsey & Bates, 1981) (Lawrence, 1982) (Myers, 1980). It is being used in vocational counseling, and a growing body of information is being collected on the preferences of different types for different kinds of work (Myers, 1980) (McCaulley, 1978) and spiritual growth (Schemel, 1982).

In the area of somatotypes, Sheldon's original work included a study of delinquent boys, and this work has been built on and continued in various ways (Cortes & Gatti, 1972) (Stewart, 1980) (Hartl, Monnelly & Elderkin, 1982). Typology also has a potentially fertile field of application in international relations. Sheldon's *Atlas of Men* could be extended to become an atlas of both men and women, country by country. Some initial work has already been done. Parnell has done extensive somatotyping of English people. Petersen produced an atlas of children made up of Dutch children of both sexes. Kraus studied the Japanese men of North Honshu, and Roberts and Bainbridge the northern Nilotics who lived in the Sudan, etc. Dupertuis' Structural Profile provides a simple yet highly effective tool to differentiate between the somatotypes of different groups, and initial measurements of groups around the world have already been taken. The Center for the Application of Psychological Type is working on an atlas of psychological type tables based on the MBTI.

Two Perspectives from Psychological Types

The principal purpose of this book has been to propose that the typologies of Jung and Sheldon can be integrated to form a powerful tool for understanding and dealing with human differences. For the most part we have incorporated Sheldon's work into Jung's broader view of the personality, and viewed psychological types in the light of C.A. Meier's statement,

"Individuation begins and ends with typology."

If we stand at the vantage point of psychological types, there are two main perspectives that open up to our view. They can be characterized as descending and ascending. The descending perspective allies psychological types with somatotypes, and proceeds from there to an examination of the biochemical and genetic aspects of human differences. We have briefly mentioned some of the contributions of Eysenck and the factor analysis school. Particularly noteworthy is Eysenck's attempt to delineate the biological basis for introversion and extraversion in terms of the reticulated activating system. There are other areas that would reward the careful attention of the Jungian or Sheldon-oriented typologists. These include the experimental work carried out by Kretschmer and his associates (Eysenck, 1951), McDougall's early article on the chemical theory of temperament which appeared in 1928, Cortes and Gatti's (1972) interesting and carefully done review of evidence in favor of the embryological basis to somatotypes and the work of people like Barchas et al. (1975) who have begun to demonstrate the genetically based intra-species variation of catecholamines in lower animals, for these same intra-species variations will probably be demonstrated before long in humans as well.

Particularly interesting is Morgan Worthy's (1975) work on the relationship between eye color and behavior. He focuses on the non-visual effects of light on the endocrine system via the pineal. Pineal functioning can be related to inhibited and reactive behavior, circadian rhythm, rate of sexual maturation and possibly sex ratio as well. (Ott, 1973). It is possible that these ideas could be linked with somatotypes via ectomorphy-introversion. The ectomorph, for example, seems to have a hypofunctional endocrine system except for the glands derived from the ectodermal tissue, one of which is the pineal. (Martiny, 1948). The ectomorph also exhibits inhibited conduct, different circadian rhythms from the extravert, and a slower rate of sexual maturation. There are also sex ratio differences between men and women of different somatotypes (Parnell, 1958, and Bernstein et al., 1961). Pineal function has also been associated with maze ability, and it would not be surprising if this were an activity the introverted intuitive types excelled at. The ancient association between the pineal and clairvoyance and meditation would then take on a different perspective. In the same way, the myth of Daedalus, the father of inventions and the inventor of the maze, and the fate of his son Icarus, could conceivably be viewed from a Jungian typological perspective. Not to be overlooked are the possible connections between the pineal and the midbrain, which appears to be the specific site of the pineal's melatonin activity (Fraschini, Collu and Martini, 1971). This might allow a connection to be made with Eysenck's theory.

Worthy also found a relationship between length and eye color in birds, and suggests that the same might be true in humans. This calls to mind the relationship between ectomorphy and height. The pineal has also been implicated in psychiatric illnesses (Mullen and Silman, 1977). Propranolol is said to decrease melatonin synthesis and have a therapeutic effect in schizophrenia, while psychotomimetic agents increase melatonin synthesis. This, too, suggests the relationship between ectomorphy and schizophrenia.

All this is simply to suggest there are many interesting areas that could be explored from a descending typological perspective. The relationship between the typologists and the biochemists could be a mutually enriching one.

There is also an ascending perspective which starts from psychological types and attempts to relate Jung's scientific methodology to the philosophy of nature, metaphysics and theology. While such a perspective seems at first highly speculative and fanciful, we have already touched briefly in chapter 7 on one important practical implication of the kind of epistemological typology we hold. There are potentially fruitful uses of analytical psychology within the religious sphere that are being impeded because a measure of epistemological ambiguity surrounds the relationship between Jung's psychology and religion. The second volume in this series will deal with these topics.

Epilogue

Individual Differences as a Contemporary Problem

The explicit study of human differences extends over 2,000 years of history and exists in many cultures, and yet the problem it embodies has not become truly conscious. Typology has often remained a small footnote in the study of medicine, or has been amalgamated with phrenology or physiognomy, or associated with racism or nationalism. This lack of consciousness in no way mitigates the detrimental effects that the ignorance of this subject has had on human relationships. Today there is the strong possibility that the question of individual differences will become more fully conscious under the impact of the physical sciences, especially genetics and biochemistry. The factual foundations to human differences will be undeniable. There are two possible responses to this new awareness. The first is to resurrect the racist mentality, and use the real fact of human differences as justification for classifying people in a heirarchy of worth, a society of have and have nots. The other possibility is that through the work of people like Sheldon and Jung, we cannot only understand the range of human differences, but avoid the pitfalls of discrimination, prejudice and projection that accompany this awareness. They allow us to see how, while being different, our development calls us towards a wholeness that transcends these differences. They safeguard both legitimate diversity and human unity.

Bibliography

Adler, G. (1961). *The Living Symbol. A Case Study in the Process of Individuation.* New York: Pantheon Books, Inc.

Allport, G. W. (1937). *Personality: A Psychological Interpretation.* New York: Holt, as cited in Hall and Lindzey, *Theories of Personality.*

Arehart-Treichel, J. (1980). *Biotypes—The Critical Link Between Your Personality and Your Health.* Time Books.

Arieti, S. (1974). *Interpretation of Schizophrenia.* Basic Books.

Barchas, J.D., Ciananello, R. D., Kessler, S., and Hamburg, D. A. (1975) "Genetic Aspects of Catecholamine Synthesis" in *Genetic Research in Psychiatry* (ed. R. R. Fieve, D. Rosenthal, and H. Brill). Baltimore: John Hopkins University Press.

Bash, K. W. (1961). *Introduction to General Clinical Psychopathology.* Zurich: C. G. Jung Institute.

Bernstein, M., Martinez, E., and Gustin, M. (May-June, 1961). "Physical and Psychological Variation and the Sex Ratio", *Journal of Heredity,* Vol. 52, no. 3, pp. 109-112.

Bisbee, C., Mullaly, R. and Osmond, H. (1982) "Type and Psychiatric Illness." *Research in Psychological Type,* (ed. T. G. Carskadon), Vol. 5, pp. 49-68.

Blake, M.J.F. (1967). "Relationship between Circadian Rhythm of Body Temperature and Introversion-Extraversion." *Nature* 215, pp. 896-897.

Bradway, K. (1964). "Jung's Psychological Types: Classification by Test vs. Classification by Self." *Journal Analyt. Psychol.* 9, 2 pp. 129-135.

Bradway, K. and Detloff, W. (1976). "Incidence of Psychological Types." *J. Analyt. Psychol.,* pp. 135-146.

Bradway, K. and Wheelwright, J. (1978). "The Psychological Type of the Analyst." *J. Analyt. Psychol.,* pp. 211-225.

Brawer, F. B. and Spiegelman, J. M. (1964). "Rorschach and Jung." *J. Analy. Psychol.,* 9, 2, pp. 137-149.

Briggs, C. and Briggs-Myers, I. (1962). *The Myers-Briggs Type Indicator* (MBTI). Center for Applications of Psychological Type, Inc., 414 Southwest 7th Terrace, Gainesville, Florida 32601, or Consulting Psychologists Press, Inc., 577 College Ave., Palo Alto, CA 94306.

Brues, A. M. (1964). "A Genetic Analysis of Human Eye Color." *Am. J. of Physical Anthro.,* 4, pp. 1-36.

_____ (1950). "Linkage of Body Build with Sex, Eye Color, and Freckling." *Am. J. of Human Genetics,* Vol.2, No. 3, pp. 215-238.

Buss, A. and Plomin, R. A. (1975). *A Temperament Theory of Personality Development.* New York: Wiley.

Buss, A. and Poley, W. (1976). *Individual Differences: Traits and Factors.* New York: Gardner Press, Inc.

Cadoret, R. J. and Winokur, G. (1976). "Genetics of Affective Disorders." *Psychiatry and Genetics* (ed. M. Sperber and L. Jarvik), Basic Books.

Capt, *Myers-Briggs Type Indicator Bibliography,* (1982) 414 Southwest 7th Terrace, Gainesville, Florida 32601

Carlson, R. (1980). "Studies of Jungian Typology: II. Representations of the Personal World." *J. of Personality and Social Psychol.,* Vol. 38, No. 5, pp. 801-810.

Cortes, J. B. and Gatti, F. M. (1965). "Physique and Self-Description of Temperament." *J. of Consulting Psychology,* Vol. 29, No. 5, pp. 432-439.

_____ (1972). *Delinquency and Crime, A Biopsychosocial Approach, Empirical, Theoretical and Practical Aspects of Criminal Behavior.* New York and London: Seminar Press.

Danby, P. M. (1953). "A Study of the Physique of Some Native East Africans." *J. Roy. Anth. Inst.* 83, pp. 194-214.

Deabler, H., Hartl, E., and Willis, C. (Oct. 1975). "Physique and Personality, Somatotype and Vocational Interest." *Perceptual and Motor Skills,* Vol. 41 (2), p. 382.

Detloff, W. "Psychological Types: Fifty Years After." *Spring,* pp. 62-73.

Diamond, D. (1957). *Personality and Temperament.* New York: Harper and Bros.

Dicks-Mireaux, M. J. (1964). "Extraversion-Introversion in Experimental Psychology." *J. Analyt. Psychol.,* pp. 117-127.

Draper, G., Dupertuis, C. W. and Caughey, Jr., J. L. (1944). *Human Constitution in Clinical Medicine.* New York: Harper and Bros.

Dubey, G. P., Agrawal, S. and Udupa, K. N. (Sept. 1968). "[131] I Profile Scan in Different Human Constitutions by Whole Body Counter." *Indian J. Med. Res.,* pp. 466-469.

Dupertuis, C. Wesley and Dupertuis, Helen S. (1968). *The Role of the Somatotype in Survivorship Among Cardiac Patients.* School of Medicine, Case Western Reserve University.

_____(1974). *The Structural Profile*. Privately circulated c/o C. Wesley Dupertuis, Case Western Reserve University, University Archives, 301 Quail Building, Cleveland, OH 44106.

Eysenck, H. J. (Dec. 1950). "Cyclothymia and Schizothymia as a Dimension of Personality. I. Historical Review." *J. of Personality*, Vol. 19. No. 2, pp. 123-152.

_____ (1956b). "The Inheritance of Intraversion-Extraversion." *Acta Psychologica*, 12, pp. 95-110.

_____(1967). *The Biological Basis of Personality*. Springfield, IL: Charles C. Thomas Publisher.

_____ (1970). (ed.) *Readings in Extraversion-Introversion. Vol. 1: Theoretical and Methodological Issues*. Vol. 2:*Fields of Application*. Vol. 3: *Bearings on Basic Psychological Processes*. New York: Wiley-Interscience.

_____(1970). *The Structure of Human Personality*. London: Methuen & Co., Ltd.

_____(Oct. 1982). "The Biological Basis of Cross-Cultural Differences in Personality: Blood Group Antigens." *Psychol. Reports*, Vol. 51 (2), pp. 531-546.

Fordham, M. (1972). "Note on Psychological Types." *J. of Analy. Psychol.*, 17, 2, pp. 111-115.

Fraschini, F., Collu, R. and Martini, L. (1971). "Mechanisms of Inhibitory Action of Pineal Principles on Gonadotropin Secretion." *The Pineal Gland*. (ed. Wolstenholme, G. E. W. and Knight, J.) Edinburgh: Churchill Livingstone, pp. 259-273.

Friedman, M. and Rosenman, R. H. (1974). *Type A Behavior and Your Heart*. New York: A Fawcett Crest Book.

Garron, D. C. (1970) "Sex-Linked, Recessive Inheritance of Spatial and Numerical Abilities, and Turner's Syndrome." *Psychol. Review*, Vol. 77, No. 2, pp. 147-152.

Gary, A. L. and Glover, J. (1976). *Eye Color, Sex and Children's Behavior*. Chicago: Nelson-Hall.

Gray, H. (Aug.-Nov. 1946). "Jung's Psychological Types in Relation to Occupation, Race, Body-Build." *Stanford Med. Bull.*, pp. 100-103.

_____(1948). "Jung's Psychological Types in Men and Women." *Stanford Med. Bull.*, 6, pp. 29-36.

Gray, H. and Wheelwright, J. B. (1946). "Jung's Psychological Types, Their Frequency of Occurrence." *J. of General Psychol.*, 34, pp. 3-17.

Groesbeck, C. J. (1978). "Psychological Types in the Analysis of the Transference." *J. of Analyt. Psychol.*, Vol. 23, pp. 23-53.

Grotevant, H., Scarr, S. and Weinberg, R. A. (1977). "Patterns of Interest Similarity in Adoptive and Biological Families." *J. of Personality and Social Psychol.*, 35 (9), pp. 667-676.

Hall, C. S. and Lindzey, G. (1970). *Theories of Personality* (2nd Ed.). New York: Wiley.

Hanson, J. R. and Silver. *Teacher Self-Assessment Manual.* Hanson Silver & Associates, Inc., Moorestown, NJ.

Hartl, E., Monnelly, E. and Elderkin, R. (1982). *Physique and Delinquent Behavior, A Thirty Year Follow-Up of W. H. Sheldon's Varieties of Delinquent Youth.* Academic Press.

Haslam, D. R. (1967). "Individual Differences in Pain Threshold and Level of Arousal." *Brit. J. of Psychol.*, 58, pp. 139-142.

Havice, D. W. (1977). *Personality Typing, Uses and Misuses.* Univ. Press of America.

Henderson, J. L. (1955). "The Inferior Function: A Study of the Application of Psychological Types in Psychotherapy." *Studien zur analytischen Psychologie* C. G. Jung, Zurich: Rascher.

Heston, L. L. (1973). "The Genetics of Schizophrenic and Schizoid Disease." *Orthomolecular Psychiatry* (Treatment of Schizophrenia), (ed. Hawkins, D. and Pauling, L.), San Francisco: W. H. Freeman and Co., pp. 54-70.

Horn, J., Plomin, R. and Rosenman, R. (1976). "Heritability of Personality Traits in Adult Male Twins." *Behavior Genetics*, 6 (1), pp. 17-30.

Humphreys, L. G. (1957). "Characteristics of Type Concepts with Special Reference to Sheldon's Typology." *Psych. Bull.* 54, pp. 218-228.

Jenkins, C. D. (1975). "The Coronary Prone Personality." *Psychological Aspects of Myocardial Infarction and Coronary Care.* (Ed. Gentry, W. D. and Williams, Jr., R. B.). Mosby.

Jung, C. G. (1913). "A Contribution to the Study of Psychological Types." *Coll. Works*, 6.

_____ (1916/1957). "The Transcendent Function." *Coll. Works*, 8.

_____ (1919). "On the Problem of Psychogenesis of Mental Disease." *Coll. Works*, 3.

_____ (1921). "Psychological Types." *Coll. Works*, 6.

_____ (1928). "The Relations Between the Ego and the Unconscious." *Coll. Works*, 7.

_____ (1929). "The Significance of Constitution and Heredity in Psychology." *Coll. Works, 8.*

_____ (1931). "A Psychological Theory of Types." *Coll. Works*, 6.

_____ (1934/1950). "A Study in the Process of Individuation." *Coll. Works*, 9, Part I.

_____ (1950). "Concerning Mandala Symbolism." *Coll. Works*, 9, Part I.

_____ (1952). "Synchronicity: An Acausal Connecting Principle." *Coll. Works*, 8.

_____ (1961). *Memories, Dreams, Reflections.* New York: Vintage Books.

_____ (1968). *Man and His Symbols.* New York: Dell.

_____ "The Symbolic Life" (Miscellaneous Writings). *Coll. Works*, 18.

_____ *Letters*, Vol. 1: 1906-1950, and Vol. 2: 1951-1961, Princeton University Press.

Kiersey, D. and Bates, M. (1978). *Please Understand Me: An Essay on Temperament Styles.* Del Mar, CA: Promethean Books.

Kline, N. S. and Tenney, A. M. (1950). "Constitutional Factors in the Prognosis of Schizophrenia." *Amer. J. Psychiat.*, 107. pp. 432-441.

Kraus, B. S. (1952). "Male Somatotypes Among the Japanese of N. Honshu." *Am. J. of Phys. Anthrop.*, 10, pp. 347-364.

Kretschmer, E. (1936). *Physique and Character, An Investigation of the Nature of Constitution and of the Theory of Temperament.* Harcourt Brace.

Laverty, S. G. (1958). "Sodium Amytal and Extraversion." *J. Neurology and Neurosurgery and Psychiatry*, 21, pp. 50-54.

Lawrence, G. (1979). *People Types & Tiger Stripes.* CAPT.

Lenski, R. (Sept. 1977). "Eye Color's Contribution to National Temperament." *Body and Mind: A Journal of Constitutional Psychology*, Vol. 1, No. 4. P. O. Box 4815, Washington, D.C. 20008.

_____ (1981). *Toward a New Science of Man, Quotations for Sociobiology.* Washington, D.C.: Pimmit Press.

Lester, D. (1981). "Ectomorphy and Suicide." *J. Social Psychol.*, pp. 135-136.

Lindzey, G. (1967). "Behavior and Morphological Variation." *Genetic Diversity and Human Behavior*, (ed. Spuhler, J. N.). Chicago: Aldine Publishing Co., pp. 227-240.

Livson, N. and McNeil, D. (1962). "Physique and Maturation Rate in Male Adolescents." *Child Development*, 33, pp. 145-152.

Loehlin, J. C., Willerman, L. and Horn, J. M. (1982). "Personality Resemblances Between Unwed Mothers and Their Adopted-Away Offspring." *J. Personality and Social Psychol.*, Vol. 42, No. 6, pp. 1089-1099.

Loomis, M. and Singer, J. *The Singer-Loomis Inventory of Personality*. Center for the Study of Cognitive Processes, Psychology Dept., Wayne State University, Detroit, MI 48202.

Loomis, M. (1982). "A New Perspective for Jung's Typology: The Singer-Loomis Inventory of Personality." *J. Analy. Psychol.*, 27, pp. 59-69.

Lynn, R. and Eysenck, H. J. (1961). "Tolerance for Pain, Extraversion and Neuroticism." *Perceptual and Motor Skills*, 12, pp. 161-162.

Mann, H., Siegler, M. and Osmond, H. (1968). "The Many Worlds of Time." *J. Analyt. Psychol.*, Vol. 13, 1, pp. 33-55.

Maritain, J. (1959). *Degrees of Knowledge*. New York: Charles Scribner's Sons.

Marshall, I. N. (1968). "The Four Functions: A Conceptual Analysis." *J. Analyt. Psychol.*, 13, 1, pp. 1-32.

Martiny, M. (1948). *Essai de Biotypologie Humaine*. Paris: Peyronnet.

McBroom, P. M. (1980). "Behavioral Genetics." *Monographs 2,* Bethesda, MD. Nat. Institute of Mental Health.

McCaulley, M. H. (1978). *Application of the Myers-Briggs Type Indicator to Medicine and Other Health Professions: Monograph I.* CAPT.

_____ (1980). *Isabel Briggs Myers: Her Life*. MBTI News.

_____ (1981). "Jung's Theory of Psychological Types and the Myers-Briggs Type Indicator." Paul McReynold, *Advances in Psychological Assessment V,* Jossey Bass, pp. 294-352.

McDougall, W. (1929). "A Chemical Theory of Temperament Applied to Introversion and Extraversion." *J. Abnorm. Soc. Psychol.*, 24, pp. 393-409.

McKusick, V. A. (1964). *On the X Chromosome of Man.* Am. Insti. of Biolog. Sciences. Baltimore, MD: Waverly Press.

McNeil, D. and Livson, N. (1963). "Maturation Rate and Body Build in Women." *Child Development*, 34, pp. 25-32.

Meier, C. A. and Wozny, M. A. (1978). "An Empirical Study of Jungian Typology." *J. Analyt. Psychol.*, 23, 3, pp. 226-230.

Meier, C. A. (1971). "Psychological Types and Individuation: A Plea for a More Scientific Approach in Jungian Psychology." *The Analytic Process, Aims, Analysis and Training.* (Ed. Wheelwright, J. B.). New York: G. P. Putnam Sons, pp. 297-308.

———————— (1983). Personal Communication.

Metzner, R. (1980). "Correlations Between Eysenck's, Jung's and Sheldon's Typologies." *Psychological Reports*, 47, pp. 343-348.

———————— (1979). *Know Your Type.* Anchor Books.

Metzner, R., Burney, C. and Mahlberg, A. (1981). "Towards a Reformulation of the Typology of Functions." *J. Analyt. Psychol.*, 26, pp. 33-47.

Mullen, P. E. and Silman, R. E. (1977). "The Pineal and Psychiatry: A Review." *Psychological Medicine*, 7, pp. 407-417.

Myers, I. B. (1962). *The Myers-Briggs Type Indicator Manual.* Palo Alto, CA: Consulting Psychologists Press.

———————— (1976 rev.) *Introduction to Type.* CAPT.

Myers, I. B. and Myers, P. B. (1980). *Gifts Differing.* Palo Alto, CA: Consulting Psychologists Press.

Myers-Briggs Type Indicator Bibliography. (1982). Center for Applications of Psychological Type, Gainesville, Florida.

Neumann, E. (1969). *Depth Psychology and a New Ethic.* New York: Harper & Row.

Oppenheim, J. (1931). *American Types: A Preface to Analytic Psychology.* New York: Knopf.

Osborne, R. H. and DeGeorge, F. V. (1959). *Genetic Basis of Morphological Variations.* Cambridge, Mass.: Harvard University Press.

Osmond, H., Siegler, M. and Smoke, R. (1977). "Typology Revisited: A New Perspective." *Psychol. Perspectives*, Vol. 8, 2, pp. 206-219.

Osmond, H. (1983). Personal Communication.

Ott, J. N. (1976). *Health and Light.* New York: Pocket Books.

Parnell, R. W. (1958). *Behavior and Physique (An Introduction to Practical and Applied Somatometry).* London: Edward Arnold.

———————— (1959). "Physique and Family Structure." *Eugenics Review,* 51, pp. 75-88.

Petersen, G. (1967). *Atlas for Somatotyping Children.* New York: Charles C. Thomas.

Plaut, A. (1972). "Analytical Psychologists and Psychological Types (Comment on Replies to a Survey)." *J. Analyt. Psychol.,* 17, 2, pp. 137-149.

Quenk, N. L. (1978-80). "On Empirical Studies of Jungian Typology." *J. Analyt. Psychol.,* pp. 219-225.

Rees, L. (1961). "Constitutional Factors and Abnormal Behavior." *Handbook of Abnor. Psychol.* (ed. Eysenck, H. J.). New York: Basic Books, pp. 344-392.

———————— (1968). "Constitutional Psychology." *International Encyclopedia of the Social Sciences,* Vol. 13 (ed. Sill, D. L.). New York: Macmillan, pp. 66-76.

Richek, H. G. and Bown, O. H. (1968). "Phenomenological Correlates of Jung's Typology." *J. Analyt. Psychol.,* Vol. 13, pp. 57-65.

Roberts, D. F. and Bainbridge, D. R. (1963). "Nilotic Physique." *Amer. J. Phys. Anthro.,* 21, pp. 341-371.

Rosenthal, D., Wender, P. H., Kety, S. S., Schulsinger, F., Welner, J. and Ostergaard, L. (1968). "Schizophrenics' Offspring Reared in Adoptive Homes." *The Transmission of Schizophrenia.* (ed. Rosenthal, D. and Kety, S. S.) Oxford: Pergamon, pp. 377-391.

Rossi, E. (1977). "The Cerebral Hemispheres in Analytical Psychology." *J. Analyt. Psychol.,* Vol. 22, pp. 32-58.

Scarr, S. (1969). "Social Introversion-Extraversion as a Heritable Response." *Child Development,* 40, pp. 823-832.

Schemel, G. J. and Borbely, J. A. (1982). *Facing Your Type.* Jesuit Center for Spiritual Growth, Wernersville, Penn.

Sheldon, W. H. (1936). *Psychology and the Promethean Will.* New York: Harper.

Sheldon, W. H. (with the collaboration of Stevens, S. S. and Tucker, W. B.) (1940). *The Varieties of Human Physique: An Introduction to Constitutional Psychology.* New York: Harper.

Sheldon, W. H. (with the collaboration of Stevens, S. S.) (1942). *The Varieties of Temperament: A Psychology of Constitutional Differences.* New York: Harper.

Sheldon, W. H. (with the collaboration of Hartl, E. M. and McDermott, E.) (1949). *Varieties of Delinquent Youth: An Introduction to Constitutional Psychiatry.* New York: Harper.

Sheldon, W. H. (with the collaboration of Dupertuis, C. W. and McDermott, E.) (1954). *Atlas of Men: A Guide for Somatotyping the Adult Male at All Ages.* New York: Harper.

Sheldon, W. H. (1963). "Constitutional Variation and Mental Health." *Encyclopedia of Mental Health*, Vol. 2. New York: Franklin Watts, pp. 355-366.

Sheldon, W. H., Lewis, N. D. C. and Tenney, A. M. (1969). "Psychotic Patterns and Physical Constitution: A Thirty-Year Follow-Up of Thirty-Eight Hundred Psychiatric Patients in New York State." *Schizophrenia: Current Concepts and Research.* (ed. D. V. Siva Sankar). New York: PJD Publications, pp. 838-912.

Sheldon, W. H. (1975). *Prometheus Revisited.* Schenkman.

Sherman, R. G. (1981). "Typology and Problems in Intimate Relationships." *Research in Psychological Type*, Vol. 4 (ed. Carskadon, T. G.), pp. 4-23.

Shields, J., Heston, L. L. and Gottesman, I. I. (1975). "Schizophrenia and the Schizoid: The Problem for Genetic Analysis." *Genetic Research in Psychiatry* (ed. Fieve, R. R., Rosenthal, D. and Brill, H.). Baltimore and London: The John Hopkins University Press, pp. 167-197.

Smith, S. L. (1968). "Extraversion and Sensory Threshold." *Psychophysiology*, 5, pp. 293-299.

Sperber, M. and Jarvik, L. (eds.). (1976). *Psychiatry and Genetics.* Basic Books.

Stafford, R. E. (1961). "Sex Differences in Spatial Visualization as Evidence of Sex-Linked Inheritance." *Perceptual and Motor Skills*, 13, p. 428.

Stewart, H. (1982). "Body Type, Personality Temperament and Psychotherapeutic Treatment of Female Adolescents." *Adolescence*, Vol. 17, No. 67.

_____ (1980). "Body Type, Personality Temperament and Pschotherapeutic Treatment of Male Adolescents." *Adolescence*, 15, 60, pp. 927-932.

Stricker, L. J. and Ross, J. (1964). "An Assessment of Some Structural Properties of the Jungian Personality Typology." *J. Abnor. and Social Psychol.*, 68, pp. 62-71.

Thomas, A. and Chess, S. B. (1977). *Temperament and Development*. New York: Mazel.

Thurstone, L. L. (1959). *The Measurement of Values*. Chicago: Uni. of Chicago Press.

Van Der Hoop, J. H. (1979). *Conscious Orientation: A Study of Personality Type in Relation to Neurosis and Psychosis*. Darby, PA: Darby Books.

Villanueva, Sagrado, Maria. (1979). *Manual de Tecnicas Somatotipologicas*. Mexico: Universidad Nacional Autonoma de Mexico.

Von Franz, M.-L. (1971). "The Inferior Function" in *Jung's Typology*. New York: Spring Publications.

Walker, R. N. (1978). "Pre-School Physique and Late-Adolescent Somatotype." *Annals of Human Biology*, 5, pp. 113-129.

Walker, R. N. and Tanner, J. M. (1980). "Prediction of Adult Sheldon Somatotype I and II from Ratings and Measurements at Childhood Ages." *Annals of Human Biology*, Vol. 7, No. 3, pp. 213-224.

Wheelwright, J. B., Wheelwright, J. H. and Buehler, J. A. (1964). *Jungian Type Survey: The Gray-Wheelwright Test Manual* (16th revision). San Francisco, Society of Jungian Analysts of Northern California.

Williams, R. J. (1956). *Biochemical Individuality: The Basis for the Genetotrophic Concept*. Texas: Univ. of Texas Press.

Winge, O. (1921). "On a Partial Sex-Linked Inheritance of Eye Colour in Man." *Compt. Rend. Lab.* Carlsberg, Copenhagen, 14: 1-4.

Winokur, G. and Tanna, V. L. (1969). "Possible Role of X-Linked Dominant Factor in Manic Depressive Disease." *Diseases of the Nervous System*, Vol. 30, pp. 89-93.

Witzig, J. S. (1978). "Jung's Typology and Classification of the Psychotherapies." *J. Analyt. Psychol.*, 23, 4, pp. 315-331.

Worthy, M. (1974). *Eye Color, Sex and Race: Keys to Human and Animal Behavior*. Anderson, S. C.: Droke House Hallux.

Index

175

eye color, 158, 160
Eysenck, H.J., 112, 148, 156, 162
Eysenck Personality Inventory, 133

factor analysis, 110, 114ff, 162
falling in love, 97ff
feeling function, 19, 26ff, 34ff, 39, 80ff, 82ff, 90
feeling, moments of high intensity, 62
fourth function, 21, 41, 58ff, 83, 142
Fraschini, F., 163
Freud, S., 18, 105
Friedman, M., 146

Garron, D., 160
Gary, A.L., 157
Gatti, F., 17, 120, 133, 143, 156, 161
genetics, 143ff, 156ff
Glover, J., 157
Gray, H., 148
Gray Wheelwright Psychological Type Test, 133
Groesbeck, C. Jess, 109

Hall, C., 113, 119
Hanson, J., 161
Hartl, Emil, 118, 135, 140, 161
Heath, B., 115
Heston, L., 153
Horn, J., 157

Icarus, 163
individuation, 60, 88, 104, 105ff, 108ff, 147, 162
Inferior Function, 41
inferior function, cf. fourth function
introversion, 19, 38ff, 90, 112
introverted feeling type, 34ff, 51ff, 82ff
introverted intuition type, 32ff, 48, 74ff, 84
introverted sensation type, 30ff, 48ff, 78ff
introverted thinking type, 35ff, 51ff, 82ff, 85, 106, 126
intuition function, 19, 24ff, 32ff, 90, 127
I.Q., 136

Japanese men, 161
Jarvik, L., 156
Jenkins, C. David, 146
Jung, C.G., 18, 41, 65ff, 104ff, 122, 124ff, 148, 150ff, 155, 156
Jung, C.G., Institute, Zurich, 41, 66,
Jung, C.G., Training Center, 66

Keirsey, D., 161
Kety, S., 153
Kline, N., 154, 156
Kraepelin, E., 149
Kraus, B., 161
Kretschmer, E., 110, 124ff, 148ff, 150, 153, 162

Laney, A., 136
Laverty, S., 112
Lawrence, G., 161
Lenski, R., 158
leptosomatic, 148
Lewis, N., 149
Lindzey, G., 113, 119
Linkage of Body Build with Sex, *Eye Color and Freckling*, 160
Living Symbol, 65
Livson, N., 118
Lynn, R., 112

Man and His Symbols, 65
mandala, 106
manic-depressive, 148ff, 151
Mann, H., 161
Maritian, Jacques, 115
Martini, L., 163
Martiny, M., 162
mathematics, 113ff
MBTI, 128, 131ff, 135ff, 161
McCaulley, M., 161
McDermott, Eugene, 113
McDougall, W., 162
McKusick, V., 157
McNeil, D., 118
Meier, C.A., 105, 108, 125, 161
Memories, Dreams, Reflections, 41
mesomorphy, 2, 3
   development, 56, 89ff
mesotonia, 8, 10ff, 43, 146

You may order copies of A TOOL FOR UNDERSTANDING
HUMAN DIFFERENCES by sending your name and address
and a check for $7.95 to:
                    Tools for Inner Growth
                         Box 520
                  Chiloquin, Oregon 97624